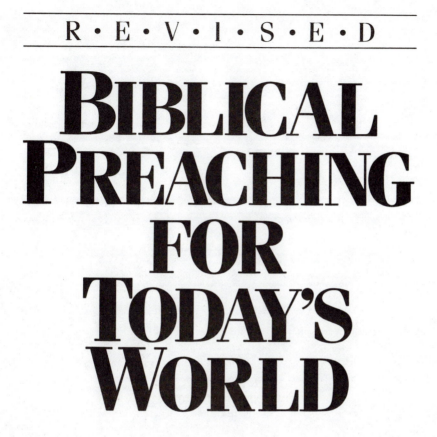

R·E·V·I·S·E·D

BIBLICAL PREACHING FOR TODAY'S WORLD

LLOYD M. PERRY

MOODY PRESS
CHICAGO

©1973, 1990 by
THE MOODY BIBLE INSTITUTE
OF CHICAGO

Library of Congress Cataloging in Publication Data

Perry, Lloyd M.
  Biblical preaching for today's world / by Lloyd M. Perry.
    p.   cm.
  ISBN 0-8024-0715-3
  1. Preaching. I. Title.
  BV4211.2.P433   1990   90-30603
  251—dc20   CIP

1 2 3 4 5 6 7 Printing/BC/Year 95 94 93 92 91 90

Dedicated to my loving wife, Elva Grace,
and to our family,
Rixson, Gregg, Joyce, William, and Cynthia Jean

CONTENTS

Persuading the Hostile Audience
Persuading the Believing Audience
The Invitations in Evangelistic Messages

FOREWORD

Communicating the Word of God to the people of God in an accurate and compelling manner is the preacher's high calling. This book provides both new and experienced preachers with the concepts, structures, and resources essential for effective biblical preaching. It is the product of many years of Dr. Perry's intensive study, gifted teaching, Spirit-directed preaching, and practical writing.

Effectiveness in the pulpit is essential for the pastor who truly loves the Lord and wants his people to hear and respond to the truth of God. This volume identifies the foundations and scriptural bases for biblical preaching, logical organizational approaches to biblical preaching, and techniques that will bring variety to preaching to enhance the listener's interest level.

This book takes a practical, hands-on approach to help preachers become effective biblical communicators. The goal is that the lives of the listeners will be both challenged and changed. Without changed lives, there can be no biblical church growth or Holy Spirit-directed revival. Biblical preaching is a cornerstone in the revitalization of the local church.

Artists work in different art forms. Preaching is an art, and like painters and sculptors, preachers can use different approaches to convey the message. Dr. Perry explains biographical, doctrinal, didactic, topical, textual, and historical approaches in a step-by-step manner to aid the preacher in varying his communication.

The people of God today need practical answers to life's daily problems and pressures. The Bible provides those answers to our personal problems. The preacher needs to be sensitive to his people's hurts and aware of what God's answers are to those needs. Chapter 6 presents the strengths and weaknesses of the life-related approach and the process to follow in preparing to meet life's situations today.

Doctrinal preaching is identified as "the culmination and crown of all sermonizing." No great stirring of the church has come without it. Doctrinal preaching teaches the people the eternal truths by statement, exposition, interpretation, and application. "So they read in the book of the law of God distinctly, and gave the sense, and caused them to understand the reading" (Neh. 8:8, KJV). Doctrinal preaching that answers the "So what?" question changes lives.

The final chapter in the book focuses on evangelism. As one layman evaluated his pastor's preaching, he told the pastor that his subject matter was superb and the organization and delivery were superior. However, the businessman went on to say, "If you were a salesman working for me, I'd fire you!" "Why?" asked the surprised preacher. "Because," replied the businessman, "after presenting me with the need and the product, you never asked for the sale." The evangelistic sermon should be biblical, direct, and fearless. It must call for action. Chapter 8 clearly presents the why and how of evangelistic sermons.

A good sermon must be biblical, logical, and practical. It must be delivered by one whose heart has been warmed by a vital and growing relationship with Jesus Christ. This volume is intended for those who are called to be heralds of truth, preachers of the gospel, ambassadors of Christ, and those who will not choose a lesser call.

GILBERT A. PETERSON
President
Lancaster Bible College
Lancaster, Pennsylvania

FOREWORD

"Well, young man, how is your devotional life?"

Lloyd Perry asked me that question when I was a freshman student at Northern Baptist Seminary and he was my faculty counselor. That was the beginning of a friendship that has enriched my life and ministry for more than forty years.

I took every course from Dr. Perry that I could fit into my schedule. I have read all of his books. I make no apology when I confess that I am devoted to "the Perry method" both in my preaching and my writing. I owe my "homiletical soul" to Lloyd M. Perry, and I wonder what I would have done had he not been my instructor and mentor.

I rejoice that Moody Press has reissued this book because it is an excellent distillation of "the Perry method." Now you, as his continuing readers, can benefit from Dr. Perry's knowledge and experience as we did in the classroom—and you won't have to take any exams!

Biblical Preaching for Today's World is almost an encyclopedia of principles and methods for the preacher who is serious about preparing biblical messages that will help people. Dr. Perry gives you no shortcuts to popular preaching, but he does teach you the disciplines necessary for the kind of preaching that brings relevance and power to the pulpit. In these pages, the beginning preacher will be introduced to classic homiletical writers whose books he ought to study; and the seasoned preacher will discover new writers and new ideas that can enhance his own ministry. There is plenty for everybody.

Best of all, Dr. Perry constantly emphasizes *the spiritual*. It is not technique alone that makes an effective preacher, but a life in contact with God, saturated with the Word, eager to share eternal truth in the power of the Holy Spirit. The author is still asking the

13

same question he asked me more than forty years ago, "Well, how is your devotional life?"

Thank you, Dr. Perry, for being faithful to your calling and to your Lord. Generations of preachers rise up to bless your name, and I am the loudest, because I owe so much to you.

WARREN W. WIERSBE
General Director
Back to the Bible
Lincoln, Nebraska

PREFACE TO REVISED EDITION

A preacher faces the God-given responsibility of presenting a changeless message to a changing world. The earlier edition of *Biblical Preaching for Today's World* was published seventeen years ago. The biblical message has not changed but the listening audience has. Therefore this volume represents a complete revision of the original.

Homiletics is, among other things, the science of sermon construction. The propositional approach is a method that provides a basic biblical and logical outline form for use in an expository, textual, or topical sermons (chapter 3). This kind of sermon construction helps the preacher in the art of sermon presentation, and helps the audience with the art of listening.

A television-oriented audience needs to see truth as well as hear it. This makes it imperative that the speaker employ the unique features of oral style, clear illustration, and practical application (chapter 5).

The biblical preacher clarifies scriptural solutions for life's difficulties and questions (life-situation preaching, chapter 6). He seeks to provide a foundation of faith (doctrinal preaching, chapter 7). He stands in the gap between a loving God and a lost world (evangelistic preaching, chapter 8). In all these kinds of preaching this book not only presents the challenge of what must be done but also how to do it. It offers a practical methodology to implement the preaching philosophy that is developed here from the Scriptures.

The sermonizer should not discard the past; he should learn from it. Throughout this volume, rather than in any one single chapter, there are references to the history of preaching and to classical rhetoric and persuasion.

Each chapter concludes with bibliographic sources for further research. These lists include books marked by asterisks to indicate the author's primary recommendations.

I am deeply indebted to several inspirational teachers of preaching: Dr. Edwin Byington, Dr. Charles Koller, and Dr. Faris Whitesell. I am also grateful for the many students who have given me the opportunity during my forty years of teaching to grow with them and to share information from my head and inspiration from my heart.

I solemnly charge you in the presence of God and of Christ Jesus, who is to judge the living and dead, and by His appearing and His kingdom: preach the word; be ready in season and out of season; reprove, rebuke, exhort, with great patience and instruction. (2 Tim. 4:1-2)

PREFACE TO ORIGINAL EDITION

This material in its original form comprised the Lyman Stewart Memorial Lectures for 1971-72, which I delivered at Talbot Theological Seminary in La Mirada, California. The design of the lecture series formed the boundaries that almost automatically excluded some material and at the same time made it imperative to include other areas.

For instance, no attempt was made to discuss and evaluate the cybernetic revolution as championed by such men as Marshall McLuhan. The science of communication has developed as a field of study in its own right. It could not be given adequate treatment within the contextual limitations of the material in this series.

The history of preaching has been overlooked by many of our present-day homileticians. Many references to great preachers and periods of great preaching are included in hopes of stimulating the preacher to survey the lives and study the sermons of some of the "preaching giants."

Some of the material in chapters 3 and 4 had been dealt with by the author in earlier publications. This coverage of the subject of sermonic arrangement was foundational for a consideration of the broad area of biblical preaching. It was therefore brought up to date and included within this lectureship.

The eighth chapter attempts to show the relevance of some of the basic concepts of speech correction and oral interpretation to the area of sermonic delivery. These have been generally omitted in previous homiletical works. Previous neglect spoke up for their inclusion here.

In compiling these lectures, I have drawn from many sources and am indebted to many students, authors, and former professors for their helpful contributions. An attempt has been made to give credit for the material within the limits of memory and research.

Omission of such credit has been by accident and not by design.

Biblical preaching has not outgrown its usefulness. The methods may vary, but the message remains the same. God's challenge and call to the preacher still comes through loud and clear: "Preach the Word."

1

BIBLICAL PREACHING AND PHILOSOPHICAL FOUNDATIONS

> Prophetic preaching does not just happen. It does not come automatically with a seminary degree, nor with the ordination to the ministry, nor with the call to the pastorate. It is not by intellectual might nor by ecstatic emotion but by the Spirit of God when He lays hold upon a preacher to deliver a life and death message to men. (Roland Leavell, *Prophetic Preaching* [Grand Rapids: Baker, 1963])

The quality of preaching always declines when the conception of preaching is removed from primary to secondary stage. However, the history of Christianity from the middle of the second century to the Reformation shows that nothing, not even elaborate ritual or ornate buildings, will suffice for the Word of God's being preached with power and reality.

We have two options. We can "curse the darkness" and let preaching stay in the swampland of mediocrity. Or we can revitalize our preaching so that God's message will get through to mankind.

Biblical preaching is still that unique method by which God through His chosen messenger reaches down into the human family and brings persons into fellowship with Himself. It employs spoken communication of divine truth for the purpose of persuasion. "With preaching Christianity stands or falls prolonging and declaring itself."[1]

The Bible is clear on the priority of preaching. The Old Testament prophets were heralds of God, declaring judgment and future hope. The New Testament uses six Greek words for preaching. John the Baptist came heralding and proclaiming (Matt. 3:1). In 1 Corinthians 5:1, Paul uses a word that means to tell good news. Other Greek words for preaching refer to bearing witness, discoursing, conversing with another, and teaching. The Great Commission commands us to go into all the world and preach the good news (Mark 16:15).

The early representatives of the Christian "Way" were not content with a religion that merely added polish to the exterior of a man. They had a religion that gave men a new heart, a new view of God, of Christ, and of their fellows, which entered every fiber of their being and colored their whole outlook on life. They believed profoundly, because they themselves knew Him, in a God who was able to turn a man round in his tracks, in fact, to *convert* him. They knew that Paul was right when he said: "If any man be in Christ, he is a new creation" (2 Cor. 5:17).

Four tests for a great speech have come down to us from classical rhetoric. The Sophists, who were the first paid public speaking teachers, trained speakers to defend their position in the land courts of the island of Sicily. They believed that a speech was worthy of high commendation providing it gained results. Plato revolted against the position of the Sophists and emphasized the fact that a speech could only be considered great if it had great truth content. Quintillian stressed the inherent quality of the life of the speaker. A speech could only be termed a great speech providing it was delivered by a good man. The Aristotelian trademark of a great speech was that it be *well organized.* It is my feeling that all four of these emphases are worthy of recognition as we try to evaluate a sermon. We trust that through the guidance of the Holy Spirit it will be used to produce constructive results. It certainly should convey truth. It should be presented by a man whose life is worthy. It is the fourth qualification to which this particular chapter is devoted. An effective biblical sermon should be marked by logical organization.

James Stewart takes a positive approach to preaching when he says,

> Do not listen to the foolish talk which suggests that, for this twentieth century, the preaching of the Word is an anachronism, and that the pulpit, having served its purpose, must now be displayed by press or radio, discussion group or Brain Trust, and finally vanish from the scene. As long as God sets His image on the soul, and men are restless till they rest in Him, so long will the preacher's task persist and his voice be heard throughout all the clamour of the world.[2]

Why is preaching, applauded by historians and exalted in Scripture, now fighting for its life? Perhaps because our practice of preaching has not been established on sound philosophical and theological foundations. Preaching is the art of which homiletics is the science and the sermon is the product. Preaching, like all other arts and sciences, must have philosophical foundations. An educational maxim declares that philosophy governs both material and methods. That is to say, we must determine the purposes of preaching, its definitions and qualifications, before we select the material to be preached and the method to be used. Our parishioners stand in desperate need of a word from God. The revitalization of preaching can come only as we clarify and reestablish our purposes for preaching and by delineating the preacher's qualifications.

PREACH WITH PURPOSE LIKE A HERALD

As a marksman aims at his target and its bull's eye and at nothing less, so the preacher must have a definite point before him that he must hit. Effective biblical preaching must be purposeful. One's philosophy, aim, or goal will govern the material that he will use and the method that he will employ. The rule is to begin with one's purpose and not with one's plan.

The present-day preacher is often guilty of preaching on small themes and temporary topics. Many of the sermons are intelligent but irrelevant. The purpose of preaching should be to meet human needs with divine power. The preacher with the aid of the Holy Spirit should aim at kindling the mind and energizing the will. He must dare to be simple but never seem shallow.

G. C. Morgan quotes Rousseau's recipe for a love letter as a recipe to be avoided in sermonizing. The recipe says: "You will begin without knowing what you are going to say and end without knowing what you have said." A sermon must in contrast to this be designed with purpose. It must be unique in its message, unique in its spirit, and must aim at godly living.

Preaching does not exist for the propagating of personal views, opinions, and social ideals. Preaching exists for the proclamation of the authoritative Word of God. The purpose of preaching is not to catch the spirit of the age but by the eternal truth and power of God to correct it. Preaching is a sacred trust, a solemn responsibility, and a divine call. The preacher must serve as a thermostat rather than a thermometer. He must have a part in setting the temperature, not merely recording it. The preacher proclaims like a herald the mighty deeds of redemption that have been accomplished and the full counsel of the divine Word that has been committed to his stewardship.

Charles Koller, who for many years was one of America's highly respected teachers of preachers, said that the preacher should so present Jesus Christ that people will come to know Him, love Him, serve Him, and yield their lives to Him.

Charles Simeon (1759-1836), one of the greatest preachers of all time, had a threefold objective in communicating the gospel. He sought with the help of the Holy Spirit to humble the sinner, to exalt the Savior, and to promote holiness in the life of the believer. Preaching that does not display divine authority both in its content and in its presentation is not the substance but only the shadow of the real thing.

To preach evangelically is an art not to be learned from books, or lectures, or inward meditation. It comes from above. It is imparted by the anointing of the Holy Spirit. To preach Christ is not merely to speak of Him but to speak as a prophet from Him. It is not by might nor by power, but by His Spirit that we are enabled to preach.

The work of the Holy Spirit in preaching may be summarized by stating that He helps the preacher in the following ways:

> He guides in finding the proper topics and Scripture passages upon which to preach.
>
> He aids in preparation by giving illumination, insight, and discernment; He aids the memory to recall parallel passages, illustrations, and ideas; He leads the preacher to find the right material.
>
> He strengthens and inspires for writing the outline.
>
> He gives additional ideas and insights to the preacher as he thinks over his message between completing the preparation and delivery of the sermon.
>
> He gives boldness and confidence at the time of delivery.
>
> He gives new thoughts and ideas, and helps forget and omit other prepared material, during delivery.
>
> He applies the Word in both expected and unexpected ways to the hearts and minds of the hearers.
>
> He unifies the audience and creates attentiveness.
>
> He convicts of sin, righteousness, and judgment and creates faith in those who hear the Word.
>
> He fixes the Word in the minds and memories of hearers, follows it up, and causes it to develop.

The early preaching was a joyous thing. Therein lay its infectiousness. The early preachers spoke with a kind of awed surprise. They could never get used to the wonder of the gospel or of the church. The joy of the early preachers sprang from the conviction that theirs was a task that taxed them to the limit and sent them back to God. It was a superhuman task and one that called for all the initiative, all the physical, mental, and spiritual discipline and stamina they could summon. The early preaching came from men who knew the meaning of the love of God.

"Who is a great preacher?" Many great preachers have been great in *one* particular aspect of the preaching task. Few have been great in many areas. If we are considering *oratory,* then we might list

Robert Hall, Thomas Guthrie, George Whitefield, Thomas Chalmers, or Charles Haddon Spurgeon. If we are considering *exposition,* we might refer to Alexander Maclaren or Sir W. Robertson Nicoll. In respect to *depth of thought,* we might name Jonathan Edwards, Samuel Hopskins, or J. H. Newman. If we are looking for great preachers in terms of their *teaching ability,* then we might note Charles Simeon of Cambridge, Frederick William Robertson of Brighton, or John Duncan of New College, Edinburgh. Great preachers from the standpoint of being great Reformers might include the names of John Knox, Andrew Melville, or Thomas Boston. We might list as one of the great preachers one who was raised in a gypsy tent, who as an unlettered lad of seventeen preached his first sermon to a group of Sunday afternoon holiday makers. He became an itinerant evangelist. He preached before kings and queens before his death in 1947 at the age of eighty-seven. Five countries have wanted to claim him as their own. He was only a converted gypsy. They called him Gypsy Smith.

PREACH WITH DIGNITY LIKE AN AMBASSADOR

We cannot separate the preacher from his preaching. A sermon that has become incarnated in a preacher who has paid the price of knowing his Bible and knowing his people can stand up to the challenge people demand of it. The preacher must show in his life that which he expounds with his lips. The Archbishop of Canterbury once asked Thomas Betterton (1635-1710) why actors seem to have no difficulty in making an impression on their audiences, whereas preachers frequently leave them cold. The famous actor replied: "Actors speak of things imaginary as if they were real, while you preachers too often speak of things real as if they were imaginary." The preacher must be a competent person in a good emotional state with a wholesome attitude toward himself, his audience, and his God.

It was Matthew Simpson, in his lectures on preaching, who stated that preaching is not merely the delivering of a message, but it is the delivery of a message by a man who professes to have felt its power and testifies to its truth in his own experience. Preaching to people is an expression of concern for them and of love for them. Love going out finds love in return.

An examination of Ephesians 4:11 and 1 Corinthians 12 will highlight some conclusions regarding the total task of the Christian minister:

As an apostle he is to challenge the will;
as a prophet he is to probe the conscience;

as an evangelist he is to woo the heart;
as a pastor he is to care for the soul;
as a teacher he is to inform the mind.[3]

The total task of the ministry demands the dedication of the total man. Preaching is not a minor matter. It is a matter of major proportions.

The Bible contains no finer characterization of the exalted nature of the minister's vocation than that of being an ambassador of Jesus Christ. As an ambassador, he is an official envoy, a diplomatic agent of the highest rank, and a resident representative of his sovereign Lord.

The biblical preacher has an appointment from God to be an ambassador for Jesus Christ. This appointment is commonly referred to as a call to preach. A firm conviction of divine call is essential to the office and gift of preaching. Such a call may be manifested in various ways but must always include the influence of the Holy Spirit. The Lord Jesus does not ask for volunteers. He appoints His ambassadors.

The appointed ambassador has been entrusted with the inerrant Word of God. His task is to bring people into agreement with Jesus Christ. Many of the ones to whom we preach are biblical illiterates. They may be well educated and sophisticated, but they need help in getting to know what the Bible says and, more especially, in coming to see how it applies to their daily living. The preacher's citizenship is not in the land where he proclaims his message but is in his heavenly homeland (Phil. 3:20).

The preacher will measure his ministry in terms of eternity rather than time (2 Cor. 5:1-4). Like the prophets of God before him, he will often sigh with anxiety but will even then take courage, for he knows that in God's good time his labor will bring its reward. When the race has been finished, the King will call the faithful runner up into the stands, and he will there receive the victor's crown.

He will measure his ministry in terms of the down payment of the Spirit of God, which he has already received (2 Cor. 5:5). Success in ministry does not come automatically with a seminary degree, ordination, or a call to a church. It comes only when the Spirit of God lays hold upon a preacher to deliver a life-and-death message to mankind.

The motivation for an effective biblical preaching ministry is twofold. On the one hand, the preacher is motivated by the desire that his ministry be acceptable to the One who has appointed him to preach. He makes it his aim to please Jesus Christ (2 Cor. 5:9*b*). On the other hand, he is motivated by his accountability. He recognizes that we must all appear before the judgment seat of Christ and give an accounting of that which we have done (2 Cor. 5:10).

The preacher proclaims God's message of reconciliation. He becomes an umpire between God and listeners (Job 9:33). The preacher has a commission to bring the two parties together. The process of this reconciliation involved God in Christ reconciling the world unto Himself, not counting the sins of people against them. The purpose is clear. Christ was made sin so that in Him we might become the righteousness of God (2 Cor. 5:21).

Donald E. Demaray closes his illuminating book *Pulpit Giants* with some summary statements about the major characteristics held in common by the twenty-five master preachers he has discussed. Among those characteristics Demaray listed were these:

> An utter seriousness about the call to preach
> A passion to communicate
> A readiness to be individual
> An eagerness to study, learn, and use the learning
> A sensitive concern for persons
> An ability to concentrate meaningfully and faithfully on their given tasks
> A healthy discontent with their own spiritual progress and ministerial success
> An honorable view of preaching as the most important activity in which they could be involved[4]

Expertness for the ministry, however, involves more than mere information. It also involves understanding: understanding people, understanding situations in which people find themselves, and understanding the relation of the biblical witness to both.

The preacher must present the gospel with boldness (1 Thess. 2:2). He must be sincere in motive so that it will be evident that he preaches to please God and not men (1 Thess. 2:3-6). When Hugh Latimer was preaching once before Henry VIII, he was overheard to say to himself as he mounted the pulpit stairs: "Latimer! Latimer! Latimer! You must take care what you say, for the great King Henry VIII is here!" Then for a moment he paused and was heard to add, "Latimer! Latimer! Latimer! You must take care what you say, for the King of kings is here!"

The preacher must be gentle in his action even as a nursing mother tenderly cares for her child (1 Thess. 2:7-9). When James Stewart of Edinburgh preached in North Morningside, the church was always filled. The people knew that the preacher loved them. The effectiveness of preaching declines when a gulf develops between the preacher and his people. His life must be marked by holiness so that he will be a good example to others (1 Thess. 2:10-

12). In his *Lectures on Preaching* Phillips Brooks said, "And first among the elements of power which make success, I must put the supreme importance of character of personal uprightness and purity impressing themselves upon the men who witness them."

Quintilian was right. The good speaker must be a good man. Saint Francis of Assisi made the same point clear when he said, "No use to go anywhere to preach unless we preach while we go."

PREACH WITH CARE LIKE A PASTOR

One of the major tests of an effective sermon centers on what happens to the individual in the pew. There should be something in every sermon for every person in the pews. No one should be sent away from church empty. The sermon is the meeting place of the soul with God. Preaching is part of the pastoral care of souls.

The pastoral precedes the prophetic. The preacher earns his right to be a prophet by faithful fulfillment of the pastoral office. The sermon must be personal to the preacher. He must speak from experience.

Preaching is divine truth voiced by a chosen personality to meet human needs. It was Charles Spurgeon who said that the sermon really begins when the application begins. A preacher who delivers a sermon without an application is like a doctor who gives a sick man a lecture on health but sends him out of the office without a prescription.

Effective biblical preaching must be characterized by being personal. Ian MacPherson has well said, "To us as sermon artists our hearers are both canvas and patrons, at once the materials on which our paintings are executed, and the public who inspect and appraise them. Hence for a double reason the people deserve our close concern."[5]

J. M. Reu wrote that "preaching is fundamentally a part of the care of souls, and the care of souls involves a thorough understanding of the congregation. The Preacher . . . must be a faithful pastor."[6] That which comes from the heart is most likely to go to the heart. Power in the pulpit comes partly through the preacher's being able to speak from experience.

Jack D. Sanford gives the essentials for a preacher as being:

> The preacher's own sure knowledge of personal salvation and
> holy calling in his own life
> A truly deep devotional life for himself
> A constant contact with men in their work-a-day world
> The spirit of self-giving and self-sacrifice

The preacher cannot change lives by eloquent hearsay. He cannot share what he does not possess or reveal what he has not seen.

Biblical truth must be preached in terms of the living experience of the listeners. A sermon involves exposition plus application. The preacher must present his message with a minimum of principles and a maximum of illustration. Effective use of visual aids, audience participation, facts, details, and examples will enhance his effectiveness with the believing listeners. He must keep his language simple and understandable.

The most effective way of getting people to do what you want them to do is to communicate your genuine love for them. A young man went to Horatius Bonar one day saying, "Dr. Bonar, I love to preach, but nothing happens when I preach." Dr. Bonar is reported to have turned and said to the young man, "But, young man, do you love people?"

Reuel Howe lists six complaints by laymen concerning preaching:

Sermons often contain too many complex ideas.
Sermons have too much analysis and too little answers.
Sermons are too formal and too impersonal.
Sermons use too much theological jargon.
Sermons are too propositional, with too little illustration.
Too many sermons simply reach a dead end and give no guidance to commitment and action.[8]

PREACH WITH POWER LIKE A PROPHET

A. J. Gordon was asked to explain the decline in the effectiveness of preaching in his day. He replied: "This decline is due, we believe, more than anything else to an ignoring of the Holy Spirit as the supreme inspirer in preaching. . . . The true preacher does not simply use the Spirit, he is used by the Spirit."[9]

The work of the Holy Spirit in preaching encompasses four stages. The first of these is the conviction of sin, righteousness, and judgment. The second stage is illumination, whereby the Spirit opens the eyes of the understanding to see Christ, the only and all-sufficient Savior. The third stage is that of regeneration, or the imparting of new life in the soul. The fourth stage is sanctification, which involves a setting apart from sin and a setting apart unto God.

Four analogies referring to the work of the Holy Spirit summarize His role in our preaching. In John 3, He is compared to wind that stirs. Acts 2 employs the analogy of fire that purifies. Isaiah 61 compares His work to oil that invigorates. The analogy in Revelation 22 compares His work to water that refreshes. Modern preaching needs the stirring, purifying, invigorating, and refreshing that come through the presence and power of the Holy Spirit. It needs the flashing eye, the pulsating song, and the vibrant enthusiasm that marked the apostles' preaching in the Spirit-filled church at Pentecost.

The way of prayer is the way of power. One who would preach with power must learn to pray alone and to pray together with others. The preacher must be known not only for his consistency, but also for his persistency, in prayer.

I stood in the evening darkness at the foot of Glacier Point in Yosemite National Park. The lights had been turned out, and I was waiting in the darkness for the avalanche of burning coals to fall from the high cliff down along the side of the valley. A voice broke the stillness of the night and cried out in the darkness, "Let the fire fall." Another voice came back through the darkness, "The fire falls." I watched the avalanche of burning fire. I will never forget the amazing sight of seeing the fire fall. I will say today as I did that night, "O God, in the darkness of our night, let the fire fall."

After a visit to the Alps, Henry Wadsworth Longfellow wrote: "Mountains are great apostles of nature whose sermons are avalanches, and whose voice is that of one crying in the wilderness."

Preacher, let's go back with our people to the mountains with the Master. Let's climb the mount of temptation in Matthew 4 and realize the importance of the Book of God. Let's take our place on the mount of teaching in Matthew 5 and find the true nature of blessedness. Let's climb the mount of transfiguration in Matthew 17 and behold the dazzling glory of Christ. Let's go out to the mount of crucifixion in Matthew 27 and grasp the importance of the blood of Christ. Let's climb the mount of triumph in Acts 1 and catch the wonder of the blessed hope. Preaching, God's method of witnessing to the world, must be revitalized. Preach with purpose as an ambassador of Christ. Preach to people in the power of the Holy Spirit of God.

George W. Truett, speaking at the C. H. Spurgeon Centenary, reminded those assembled for that occasion of an essential truth that Spurgeon believed. "[Spurgeon believed there was] no substitute for the Christian pulpit. Not the press with all its triumphs; nor the schools with all their learning; nor the amazing triumphs of science can take the place of Christ's preacher. 'For after that in the wisdom of God the world by wisdom knew not God, it pleased God by the foolishness of preaching to save them that believe.' "

Truett went on to say:

Nor will history let us forget that the halcyon days of Christianity have always been the days of great preachers and faithful preaching. It was so in the days of Tertullian, Chrysostom, Augustine, and Ambrose. It was so in the days of Luther, Calvin, Latimer, and Jonathan Edwards. It was so in the days of Spurgeon. The dry bones of the valley have ever lived and been clothed with flesh and blood when the right kind of man with the right kind of message has stood in the Christian pulpit. The moral and spiritual safety of a nation and of a world is largely within the keeping of the Christian pulpit. The Thermopylae of Christianity is the pulpit.[10]

Following a systematic method for constructing a sermon does not rule out nor does it limit the guidance of the Holy Spirit. Orderliness, not confusion, is the evidence of the leading of the Holy Spirit.

NOTES

1. P. T. Forsyth, *Positive Preaching and the Modern Mind* (Grand Rapids: Eerdmans, 1964), p. 5.
2. James Stewart, *Heralds of God* (Grand Rapids: Baker, 1972), p. 55.
3. Ian MacPherson, *The Burden of the Lord* (Nashville: Abingdon, 1957), p. 75.
4. Donald E. Demaray, *Pulpit Giants* (Chicago: Moody, 1973), pp. 165-74.
5. Ian MacPherson, *The Art of Illustrating Sermons* (Grand Rapids: Baker, 1976), p. 186.
6. J. M. Reu, *Homiletics* (Grand Rapids: Baker, 1967), p. 129.
7. Jack D. Sanford, *Make Your Preaching Relevant* (Nashville: Broadman, 1963), pp. 79-80.
8. Reuel Howe, *Partners in Preaching* (New York: Seabury, 1967), pp. 26-33.
9. Faris D. Whitesell, *Power in Expository Preaching* (Westwood, N. J.: Revell, 1963), p. 141.
10. George W. Truett, *The Inspiration of Ideals* (Grand Rapids: Eerdmans, 1950), pp. 157-58.

BIBLIOGRAPHY

Adams, Jay Edward. *Essays on Biblical Preaching.* Grand Rapids: Zondervan; Ministry Resources Library, 1986.

——————. *Preaching with Purpose.* Grand Rapids: Baker, 1982.

Blackwood, Andrew. *The Fine Art of Preaching.* New York: Macmillan, 1937.

Daane, James. *Preaching with Confidence: A Theological Essay on the Power of the Pulpit.* Grand Rapids: Eerdmans, 1980.

Demaray, Donald E. *Pulpit Giants.* Chicago: Moody, 1973.

Haselden, Kyle. *The Urgency of Preaching.* New York: Harper & Row, 1963.

* Holland, DeWitte T. *The Preaching Tradition: A Brief History.* Nashville: Abingdon; Abingdon Preacher's Library, 1980.

Jabusch, Willard F. *The Person in the Pulpit: Preaching as Caring.* Nashville: Abingdon; Abingdon Preacher's Library, 1980.

Jowett, John H. *The Preacher: His Life and Work.* New York: Harper & Row, 1912.

Kidder, Daniel P. *A Treatise on Homiletics.* New York: Carlton & Lanahan, 1866.

Lewis, Ralph L., and Gregg Lewis. *Inductive Preaching: Helping People Listen.* Westchester, Ill.: Crossway, 1983.

Liefield, Walter L. *New Testament Exposition: From Text to Sermon.* Grand Rapids: Zondervan, 1984.

* Logan, Samuel T., Jr., ed. *The Preacher and Preaching: Reviving the Art in the Twentieth Century.* Phillipsburg, N.J.: Presbyterian and Reformed, 1986.

Miller, Donald G. *The Way to Biblical Preaching.* Nashville: Abingdon, 1957.

Morgan, G. Campbell. *Preaching.* New York: Revell, 1937.

* Stewart, James S. *Heralds of God.* Reprint. Grand Rapids: Baker, 1972.

Wardlaw, Don W., ed. *Preaching Biblically.* Philadelphia: Westminster, 1983.

Weatherspoon, Jesse Burton. *Sent Forth to Preach: Studies in Apostolic Preaching.* New York: Harper & Bros., 1954.

Wiersbe, Warren W., and Lloyd M. Perry. *The Wycliffe Handbook of Preaching and Preachers.* Chicago: Moody, 1984.

2

BIBLICAL PREACHING AND BIBLICAL ORIENTATION

> Knowing the need, he must then seek his message. Here again inclusively he is never at loss. That by which a man lives, in the deepest of his life, is the Word of God. But the incidental application must be as varied as is the incidental expression; and he who would preach the Word prevailingly must live with the Word; he must know the Word of God as well as the human spirit. His business must be to know the remedy for the Need he addresses. (G. Campbell Morgan, *The Ministry of the Word* [Grand Rapids: Baker, 1970], pp. 208-9)

The Bible is the unique source and fountainhead of Christian preaching. An emphasis upon such subjects as current events, patriotic occasions, denominational issues, or psychological problems, without giving comprehensive biblical support, will mean loss both to the preacher and his congregation. The preacher cannot provide adequate biblical support without having a comprehensive grasp of the Bible. He cannot preach the "word" of God unless he knows the Word of God. A program of Bible study is indispensable so far as the preacher is concerned.

Since the Bible is God's unique communication of Himself and His truth to people, and is the highest and holiest source of truth, light, and power, there is no reason for preachers to depart from Bible preaching. The purpose of ordination is to set men apart to preach the Word of God.

The preacher is God's prophet declaring God's message to people, rather than a priest officiating at an altar on their behalf. When people go to church, they expect to hear the Bible interpreted and applied to life.

Biblical preaching is preaching with sound biblical support, molded throughout by the teachings and spirit of the Bible. No other preaching is worth the time and effort of God's spokesmen.

The Bible itself is a book of varied literary forms and tends to yield variety in the presentation of truth. It is a divine library of sixty-six volumes containing law, history, poetry, prophecy, wisdom literature, narratives, allegories, parables, apocalypses, biographies, chronicles, dramas, riddles, visions, sermons, songs, conversations, letters, and teachings. The 1,189 chapters, 31,176 verses, 14,388 Greek and Hebrew words, and 2,930 Bible characters provide adequate resource material for the sermons of a lifetime. Threescore and ten years is not time enough to allow the biblical preacher to exhaust the depths of the Bible. The more a man preaches the Bible, the more he will wish to preach it. The deeper he goes into it, and the longer he stays with it, the more he will see in it to preach.

Preaching Directed by Hermeneutics

A discussion of responsible biblical interpretation falls naturally into three divisions: the preacher himself; the Bible from which the preacher derives his message; and the people to whom he preaches.

OBSERVING EXEGETICAL PROCEDURE

Hermeneutics starts the moment the preacher closes his study door, because he himself is the first problem confronted in sermon building. The problem is called *eisegesis*, which means that the interpreter brings with him "notions, questions, interests, and a definite mind-set," which predispose him to certain ways of thinking.[1]

Exegesis is listening intently to what the Bible has to say to the preacher before he says it to the people.

John Wesley speaks to this point in a hard-hitting address to the preachers working under him:

> How much shall I suffer in my usefulness, if I have wasted opportunities . . . and droned away precious hours . . . if I have loitered away the time in which I might have become acquainted with the treasuries of sacred knowledge? . . . Have I used all possible diligence to receive the most accurate knowledge of the English Scripture? . . . Have I . . . attained a thorough knowledge of the sacred text . . . of its literal and spiritual meaning? Otherwise, how can I attempt to instruct others therein? Without this, I am a blind guide indeed. I am absolutely incapable of teaching my flock what I have never learned myself; no more fit to lead souls to God, than I am to govern the world.[2]

The purpose of exegesis is to discover and expound the true meaning of the sacred books; the process is a commitment of time, research, comparison of texts, sorting and sifting, resolving conflicts among translations, and appreciating various interpretations of Scripture scholars.

The preacher's task is to discover the true meaning of the revealed word as the Spirit of God guided the scribe who wrote the words. Original language studies are basic to an understanding of the Scripture. If the preacher uses Greek and Hebrew words in the pulpit, whether to demonstrate his expertness or simply to a misguided attempt to "clarify" a difficult text, he has missed the point. Charles R. Brown wrote, "The expository sermon is not a product of exegesis, but an exhibition of it. It is altogether wise to dig beforehand with your Greek spade and your Hebrew shovel but not to be digging while you are preaching."[3]

Most preachers are not professional exegetes, but their courses in Scripture give enough instruction and experience so they will know where they may go for help in interpreting the Scriptures for homiletic use. Exegesis will help the preacher narrow down certain topics for preaching purposes. It will give him an idea for a sermon that reflects the integrity of the passage. The preacher will, with a context of meaning derived from exegesis, emphasize the intent of the writer rather than focus on an isolated word that may not, in fact, have been the intention of the writer at all.

Remembering that interpretation is for communication, the question needs to be constantly raised, Are we getting the message through? C. S. Lewis once said that in his opinion every ministerial student, before being granted a degree, should have to take an especially important and difficult theological chapter and translate it into language the ordinary layman could understand.

Charles Haddon Spurgeon (1834-1892), whose pulpit ministry and sermonic process were universally applauded, both showed and taught his ministerial students in his Pastors' College the principles of preaching, and in exemplary fashion. Talking about sermons in one of his Friday lectures to the seminarians, Spurgeon advised: "We do not enter the pulpit to talk for talk's sake, and we cannot afford to utter pretty nothings. . . . The true minister of Christ knows that the true value of a sermon must lie, not in its fashion and manner, but in the truth it contains."[4]

W. E. Sangster, in his *Craft of Sermon Construction,* treated sermons along three lines of difference: their subject matter (content), their structural type (arrangement or design), and their psychological method (how the preacher seeks to "put it over"). However classified, sermonic elements do tend to overlap, making for mixed categories more often than not. "The ideal sermon will be as biblical in content and as functional in meeting a definite need as possible."[5]

There are three steps involved in surveying the context or background of the Scripture passage. A quotation by Don Wagner, speaking of G. Campbell Morgan's method, is helpful at this point.

> *The first step is to survey the group of Bible books in which the particular passage is located.* For example, if you were preaching on a passage in the book of Ephesians, you would want to get a general grasp of the dates, emphases, and features of the four prison epistles of which Ephesians is one. A good book of Bible introduction will help provide information for the preacher at this point. The two books, *New Testament Survey,* by Merrill Tenney, and *Bible Survey Outlines,* by Roland Hudson, will prove helpful.
>
> *The second step is to survey the particular Bible book in which the preaching portion is located.* Answering the following questions will prove helpful.

1. What is the main theme of the Bible book? Read and reread it until the main teaching can be crystallized in your thinking, and then summarize it in a sentence.
2. What can you learn about the writer of the Bible book?
3. To whom was the book originally sent?
4. Are there any particular or important repeated terms in the book?
5. What does this book teach about God?
6. What is the nature of the general content of the book? Is it argumentation, exhortation, or instruction?
7. Are there evidences within the book of manners and customs of those to whom it was written?

It is helpful for the sermonizer to formulate a broad, general outline of the book, giving special attention to changes of subject matter, personalities, and places that may help in the determination of the outline.

In order to discover similarities in outline divisions, the preacher ought to compare several outlines that others have formulated. These outlines can be compared by arranging them side by side in chart form.

The third step is to survey the context of the preaching portion itself. Charles Koller in *Expository Preaching Without Notes* has listed seven items that he terms factual data. The speaker should check each of these seven items. When he has discovered the material he wants, he should collect it and keep it in written form, both for use in the immediate sermon, and for future reference.

The items of factual data represent the absolute minimum of

work the preacher must do in preparing a passage for preaching or teaching. The following steps are essential.

1. He should first determine the speaker or writer of the passage. The kind of person represented by the writer may give a valuable clue to the major thrust of the passage and its possible application.
2. He should then determine the ones to whom the passage was first addressed. The kind of person or group who first received the message may be discovered in the congregation to which the preacher is scheduled to present this particular sermon.
3. Establish an approximate time for the incident or for the presentation of the original message. The homiletician will want to list other significant biblical and extrabiblical events that took place just before and after this particular occasion.
4. He will want to locate the place where the incident took place or where the passage was presented. It should be helpful to list other significant events that took place at the same time or nearby locations.
5. Then clarify the occasion that prompted the contents of this passage. Similar conditions may exist for the ones to receive the present sermon.
6. He will then want to determine the aim or purpose behind the passage. Is the purpose relevant to the lives of the listeners today?
7. Then formulate the main theme of the passage—a phrase that summarizes its content.

This three-step survey of the context can be illustrated by three concentric circles. The outer circle would represent the group of Bible books; the second circle the particular Bible book in which the passage is located; and the third and smallest circle the actual passage upon which one is speaking.

Studying a passage for its meaning involves not only a study of its context but also a study of its content. This content analysis involves four *procedures.*

Read the passage in several translations. Each time he reads the passage the speaker pursues a different purpose in search of message material.

The first reading should be made to determine the dominant impression gained from the message. Having preserved the main impression on paper, he reads it again in order to discover the major and minor personages, and that which is said about each one.

The preacher then turns to his third reading in order to note significant, repeated words and phrases. If he has the original languages available for his use, it would be helpful to use either his

Greek or Hebrew at this reading. In the fourth reading he seeks to determine a distinctive name or title for the passage.

The fifth reading should be done to prepare the passage for public reading from the pulpit. The passage on which the speaker is to speak should be the passage he reads as the Scripture lesson during the worship service.

Formulate an analytical outline of the passage. The paragraph divisions will indicate possible breaking points for such an outline. As the preacher makes this outline, no attempt should be made to rearrange the order of contents within the passage. Major and supporting ideas should be formulated in wording as nearly scriptural as possible and arranged so that a logical relationship may be evident. The following writers provide help in formulating such analytical outlines: Merrill Tenney, G. Campbell Morgan, W. H. Griffith Thomas, Roy Laurin, Guy King, and Lehman Strauss.

Compare parallel passages. The next procedure would be to make a comparative study of parallel passages. In doing this the speaker will note any significant additions or deletions. This kind of study will be especially relevant when preaching on the gospels. There is also in print a harmony by Crockett covering the books of Samuel, Kings, and Chronicles, which may prove helpful.

Make a grammatical survey. As the speaker formulates the grammatical survey, he should proceed to diagram according to the rules of standard grammar and syntax the ideas within the passage. This will help to clarify the logical relationship between the ideas. This process is called thematic diagramming and is illustrated on pages 256-60 of *How to Search the Scriptures*.

1. Punctuation marks. These were not in the original manuscripts. They were added by translators to help convey meaning and to clarify series of declarations, explanations, or questions. These may provide suggestions for preaching points when it comes time to formulate the sermonic outline.

2. Etymology of words. The study of word etymology will provide sermon illustration material. The meaning of a word can be made more relevant by checking the connotation of the word. The context often clarifies the meaning.

3. Verb tenses. Because they have a greater significance in the Greek and the Hebrew than they have in the general English translations, verb tenses should be noted. There are two translations that will help the student who, at this point, is handicapped by not knowing the original languages. One translation is by Helen Montgomery and is entitled *The Centenary Translation of the New Testa-*

ment. The second is the one produced by Charles Williams, entitled *The New Testament.*

4. Word order. It is profitable to check the word order in the original language. In the Greek language, for instance, the emphatic words come first in the sentence. If the sermonizer does not have at hand a ready usage of the original languages, he may profit by owning and using an interlinear Greek-English New Testament such as the one published by Zondervan and edited by Alfred Marshall. There is also an interlinear Old Testament published by Zondervan and edited by John Kohlenberger.

5. Figures of speech. Check the meaning of any figures of speech in the passage. These appear in abundance in the Scriptures, and each one within the particular passage should be identified and clarified as to its meaning and implications. Repeated, peculiar, or distinctive terms may have significance for message construction.

PREACHING CONTROLLED BY HOMILETICS

There are two kinds of preparation for a sermon. The first of these is "habitual" preparation, which is *general* in nature; and the second is "actual" preparation, which is *specific* in that it is for a specific sermon.

GENERAL HOMILETICAL PREPARATIONS

Personal growth of the preacher. General preparation involves systematic and general culture. The preacher makes himself increasingly familiar with the great subjects that belong to religion and its expression. The open secret of the success of many preachers is that they put their strength and time into the toil of collecting suitable materials for discourse. The Spirit's presence will not in the least absolve us from the need of complete preparation.

The vital thing, whether in preparation for the ministry or in the actual work of the ministry, is not the number of sermons one makes but the kind they are and the work they are fitted to do. The preacher must work at "quality control" constantly. He must do this through his own personal growth as well as individual sermon production.

The minister will grow through his own independent observation and reflection. He will grow by travel in his own land and in other lands. He will grow by the experiences of life and death, by the sins and the sorrows, the struggles and the defeats, the triumphs and the glories, in which he will either personally participate or sympathetically share.

The rightly used mind will perpetually become more and more productive by the process. Growth precedes glory, climbing precedes climax, and preparation precedes the peaks.

In order to prepare speeches it is essential for the speaker to prepare himself. He should cultivate the gift of conversation. He should acquire an appreciation for the beautiful. He will want to keep himself physically fit.

Diligent study of the preacher. From the beginning of his ministry the preacher should have a definite early morning time to enter his study. Not less than four hours each day, and as many more as possible, should be devoted to the work in this dedicated task.

Certain hours will be set aside for Bible study, certain hours for collateral reading, and certain hours for the systematic study of history, theology, philosophy, or other great fields.

The study should be the *sanctum sanctorum* of the minister's personal life.

He should establish the habit of beginning the day with a time devoted to Bible reading for the refreshment of his own soul, and in the practice of the presence of God for his own spiritual upbuilding.

During his college days the preacher should be sermonizing even though he does not have a regular church. The earlier he starts reading, praying, traveling, and living with sermonizing in mind, the greater preacher he will become.

If a man takes advantage of these quieter days when he is beginning, he will do much to get his soul and his mind ready for the larger opportunities when they come.

There are three general sources to which the speaker may go for sermon material. These are observation, reading, and conversation. The following is a list of some sources:

The Bible	Theology
Classics	Books in general
Biography	Psychology
History	Poetry
Fiction	Orations
Newspapers	Periodicals
Nature	Contemporary life
Philosophy	Sermons
Personal experience	Drama
Hymns	Science

SPECIAL HOMILETICAL PREPARATION

Specific preparation for preaching is confined to the content of the particular sermon to be preached. It involves the development of materials of the discourse, and it includes the method of outlining and writing the entire sermon.

Making orientation queries. In the process of preparing the sermon the preacher will do well to ask the following questions:

What is my chief purpose in preaching the sermon?
By what line of thought do I expect to acomplish this purpose?
How does each thought in the sermon aid in achieving this purpose?
What is the outstanding section in the sermon?
How do the other sections compare with each other in importance?
How do all the parts in the sermon compare in importance?
Does the sermon build to an intellectual climax?
Does the sermon build to an emotional climax?

Manuscripting sermonic material. Writing develops self-discipline and stimulates thinking. It increases the preacher's vocabulary. It secures to him the means of profiting by his past labors. Even if the preacher never uses his manuscript in the pulpit, the greater condensation, clarity, and picturesqueness gained through writing will prove profitable.

Observing special principles. If the homiletician were to formulate a series of steps to follow in the process of specific preparation, some of the following items probably should be included.

The one most commonly referred to is prayer and meditation. Prayer is a vital part of our spiritual preparation, but there is no need to pray that we will preach well if we have no real sermon to preach.
The sermon subject should be determined in the mind of the sermonizer at an early date.
The homiletician should, if possible, read the text in the original languages. He should also study the preaching passage in several translations.
Commentaries and books of sermons make up the last of the sources to be consulted in the process of specific preparation.

Other principles involved in the process of specific preparation for presentation should include the following:

Do not memorize the whole manuscript. Memorize the ideas.
Take painstaking care in the whole process.

Use intensive research.

Let love of serving Jesus be the ruling spirit in preparation.

Conceive of your major business as being the preaching of Christ.

Make sure the parts of the sermon are comprehensive, integrated, and progressive.

Bring the truth to bear on life situations.

Reason, remember, and relax.

Take notes while reading.

The sermon should be practiced aloud prior to delivery before a congregation.

Jordan quotes R. W. Dale and suggests a list of questions that each minister should take time to ask:

1. Does my sermon contain enough positive Christian truth to give it the power of the gospel?

2. Do I have the moral right to hope that this message will persuade people in the congregation to believe in Christianity and do something about its eternal issues?

3. Is my language plain enough and are my ideas sufficiently clear for my hearers to understand what I am trying to say?

4. Does this sermon have propelling power, that is, power enough to create desire? Is the truth, by nature and method of presentation, impelling?

5. Is everything in this messsage in harmony with the purpose and spirit of Christ?[6]

Good preaching is the product of great study. One noted preacher gained poise and power in the pulpit by putting in an hour of study for every hundred words he wrote in his sermon.

The following specific practices have been followed by some of the great preachers: John Bright read the poets for the enrichment of his style; Henry Parry Liddon read a sermon a day for years and mastered the thought and method of Jacques B. Bossuet, Jean Baptiste Massillon, and Friedrich Schleiermacher; Phillips Brooks read and reread F. W. Robertson, Horace Bushnell, James Martineau, J. F. D. Maurice, and others; and J. H. Jowett gave careful study to all his great English-speaking contemporaries in order to correct his one-sidedness in dealing with his themes.

Maintaining essential standards. There are three general marks of a biblical message that must characterize message preparation as well as message presentation.

The first of these is *accuracy*. This must be demonstrated and not just be a high resolve. The preacher must be honest and painstaking in interpretation and must also teach his people to test his messages for accuracy. He should do everything possible to avoid the credibility gap. It will take time in preparation to apply the interpretation principle of history to determine the original sense, and the interpretation principles of harmony to determine the contextual sense. Believing as we do that the Bible is the Word of God, we do not dare nor do we desire to handle it lightly and carelessly.

The second mark of a biblical message is *relevancy.* In the process of preparation the preacher must think himself into the passage he is studying. Messages must have two points of anchorage: God's Word and God's world.

The biblical message has for its third mark *authority.* The gospel of Christ is not up for debate. It demands proclamation. The preacher must make it clear that his message is taken from the Bible and not a personal message read into the Bible. It is his task to declare dogma, but not in dogmatism, which betrays arrogance. The speaker and his listeners must be able to distinguish between revelation and speculation.

Selecting sermon passages. The beginning preacher will be tempted to select a very short passage of Scripture to use as a basis for his message. This is not advocated. Such a procedure limits the sermonizer in developing his subject. By using short passages, he will find it difficult to give his people an adequate coverage of Bible content within the limited time of his pastorate.

Begin to sermonize with a larger portion, such as a chapter. As the context and content is surveyed, the Holy Spirit will often direct the sermonizer to restrict his message to just one section of the larger portion.

Determining message subjects. Sometimes a message begins with a subject rather than a passage of Scripture. There are several factors that may provide assistance in making a determination of such a subject.

The first of these is the *congregational factor.* Through personal contacts in counseling, conversation, and visitation, certain subjects may come to the surface. Preachers are encouraged to listen to people. God gave us two ears and only one mouth, which some have taken to mean that we should listen twice as much as we speak.

The second factor is the *personal factor.* The study of the Scriptures provides personal help to the speaker on his personal problems. After one has read a passage of Scripture it is wise to stop and pray, "Lord, what are you trying to tell me through this Scripture portion?"

The third factor is the *contemporaneous factor.* There may be happenings of community or national import that cry out for treatment from the Word of God. Great issues are being debated. Great problems face the world. "Is there any word from the Lord?"

If the preacher starts with a subject rather than a passage of Scripture, he has the responsibility of relating that subject to one or more passages of Scripture.

Analyzing sermon themes. The sermonizer should ask himself whether this theme is *biographical, doctrinal,* or *ethical* in nature. A theme analysis should then be made according to one of the following lists under the appropriate category.

Biographical:
What is the meaning of the individual's name?
What is the ancestral background?
What significant religious and secular crises occurred in this life?
What advantages for personal development were enjoyed?
What traits of character were manifested?
What important friendships did this person have?
What important influences did this individual exert?
What failures and faults occurred in this life?
What important contributions were made?
What main lesson does the person's life teach?

Doctrinal:
What is the definition of the terms of the theme? Check the etymology, Bible usage, and nonbiblical usage.
What is the importance of this doctrine in the light of the whole pattern of biblical truth?
What will be the results of the operation of this truth in personal experience?
How is personal faith related to this doctrine?

Ethical:
What is the definition of the terms of the theme—etymological, biblical and nonbiblical, negation, quotations from great writers, synonyms and antonyms?
When this ethical principle prevails, what relationship does it establish between the individual and God, and between the individual and his fellow man?
How can this ethical principle be realized in the individual's experience?
What is the relationship to other ethical principles?

Discovering sermon starters. The preacher must strive to develop a homiletical mind. Such a mind alerts him to sermon "starters" and sermonic material.

The process of discovering material is rhetorically called the process of invention. His ability to discover preaching possibilities will increase as he develops this homiletical mind. Some of the sermon material may be useful as illustrations within a sermon. Sensing the relevance of Bible material for sermonic purposes depends largely upon the preacher's knowledge of sermon construction methodology.

Analyzing sermon passages. You, as preacher, need to relate the subject that appears to be predominant in the passage to the whole passage by determining whether the *when, where, why, who, wherefore, what,* or *how* of your subject is being discussed. If more than one of these is discussed in the passage, which appears to have the preeminence? Be sure that you can convince yourself and your audience that this is the predominant subject of the passage. The subject is often one word that is the core of the passage and of the sermon.

Give special attention to the paragraph divisions. A good paragraph has one main idea. Find that main idea in each paragraph and relate it to the subject of the entire passage. One of the paragraphs may provide the basis for a conclusion, or another may provide the basis for a main point of the message.

If your preaching message deals with an incident, determine the steps involved in the unfolding of that incident. These steps may yield the basic idea for the main points of a sermon.

From the standpoint of human reason, why should this passage be included within the scope of the Bible? The preacher's answer to this question may help to show the revelance of this passage to present-day living.

Are there verses within the preaching portion that are regarded by many as familiar verses? These verses, which already stand out in the minds of many of the listeners, may serve as the scriptural bases for main points in the sermon. One of these familiar verses may also give the key to the major thought emphasis of the passage.

If the passage covers a period of time, determine the time order in the passage and the events pertaining to each period. If the passage deals with events that take place over a wide geographical area, determine the directional sequences within the preaching portion.

Are there cause and effect relationships within the passage? These may give helpful clues toward possible key words for the sermon.

Using resource helps. It is necessary for the sermonizer to have books at his disposal that will provide help in the preparation of messages. At this point we refer to those books that will assist in obtaining background material and inspirational ideas.

There are at least three kinds of commentaries. Each kind serves a purpose for the speaker.

The first is the critical commentary. One of the best examples is Keil and Delitzsch's work on the Old Testament.

The second is the homiletical commentary. One of these might be the *Pulpit Commentary,* and another might be Johann Petter Lange's work. This kind of commentary provides some critical information, but it also gives some sermonic suggestions.

The third kind of commentary might be called the devotional. Matthew Henry's work would be an illustration, as would Alexander Maclaren's commentary.

When beginning one's library, it is wise to purchase one set of homiletical commentaries covering the entire Bible. The sermonizer can then proceed to purchase commentaries on particular Bible books. Some speakers present series of messages on one Bible book or on a group of books. They therefore purchase several helpful works on that particular section of the Bible. This specializing in purchasing books for immediate use protects the preacher's book budget.

The primary source of materials for the sermon is the Bible. But some ideas, thoughts, and illustrations in the sermon will come from other sources. Literature, history, science, and personal experience will suggest ideas and illustrations to help make the sermon intelligible and appealing to the hearer.

When giving consideration to the possible purchase of a book for his sermon library, the preacher should ask, among other things, if the author has had experience in preaching and, therefore, if he writes from the point of view of a preacher. Biblical and critical information without spiritual inspiration will tend to produce lectures rather than sermons. Such writers as G. Campbell Morgan, W. A. Criswell, Charles L. Allen, Clovis G. Chappel, Clarence Macartney, W. Graham Scroggie, Guy King, Roy Laurin, and others have produced some homiletically productive books.

Ralph W. Sockman describes his method by saying that he sowed the ideas for his sermons in the summer and returned to his work in the fall with seventy-five or a hundred sermon themes in mind. He then frequently went over these to see "which ones seem to be sprouting."[7] He devoted three days of the week to the sermon he was to preach on Sunday morning, putting in approximately eighteen hours of study on each sermon. He consulted books in his library dealing with the sermon. When this material had been gathered, he then proceeded to organize the sermon outline. This he did on Friday night, leaving the writing of the sermon to Saturday.

R. G. Lee began, as he expressed it, by reading the Bible "with prayer in my heart that God will direct me to the choice of a subject and text upon which to pitch my mental tent." When the subject and text were chosen, he then developed an outline, doing the "best thinking I can on the passage." In doing so he searched the Bible for "substantiating statements of God's truth."[8]

When this was done, he read what other men had said about the subject, but he said, "I'm not a slave to commentaries."[9] This study was followed by the gathering of related truths from any realm: history, biography, poetry, philosophy. He even sought statements that were contrary to his own convictions. He then tried to prepare his sermons with the needs of people in mind: lost people, brokenhearted people, people in despair, complacent people. He attempted also to prepare all sermons with Jesus as the central theme and often asked himself the question: "What does Jesus think of this?" With this background of preparation in hand he then wrote his sermon in full.

H. Guy Moore speaks of a "seed plot" for future sermons. This is a drawer where he places ideas, sermons, parts of series, and illustrations as they come to him.[10]

C. Roy Angell speaks of a clipboard in his study on which he writes at the top of a blank page a text, an incident, a sermon topic that has occurred to him. Sometimes he may have as many as fifty pages on this clipboard. He goes over these each week prayerfully waiting for guidance in selecting one for a future sermon.[11]

Duke McCall says that when an insight, idea, or message grips him and fires his imagination he immediately writes it down. Sometimes he dictates a page or two to enlarge the idea. Such material is placed in a folder "where it may stay for a few days or a few years until a preaching opportunity seems to be the suitable occasion for the sermon."[12]

Applying the message. As the sermonizer studies the passage for sermon ideas, he will do well to ask himself this question: What practical advice is there within this passage that will help me in daily living? Once the sermonizer finds within the passage that which has relevance for his daily living and that which grips his own soul, he will find it easier to share the truth of that passage with those to whom he will be speaking. He will then begin to sense that which prompted John Bunyan to say, "I preached what I felt; what I smartingly did feel." Both in preaching and in praying we should feel that there is something that must be declared.

Surely, few royal figures have crammed so much into so short a life span as King Edward VI of England, son of Henry VIII. Born in 1537, he died in 1553, not quite sixteen. At nine years of age, on the occasion of his accession to the throne, he made history. On February 20, 1547, after the ceremony in Westminster Abbey, the boy king was walking in procession toward Westminster Hall where a banquet had been prepared. Just in front of him were officers of state bearing aloft three great swords. He asked what this meant, and they told him the swords stood respectively for each of the three kingdoms under his crown. "One is wanting," he exclaimed. "The Bible, the sword of the Spirit!" And he ordered that the large pulpit Bible should be taken from the lectern in the abbey and carried with solemn dignity ahead of the symbols of world power. Thus to this day the presentation of a copy of Scripture to the sovereign is part of the English coronation service.

NOTES

1. Neil B. Wiseman, comp., *Biblical Preaching for Contemporary Man* (Kansas City: Beacon Hill, 1976), p. 31.
2. Ibid, p. 38.
3. Charles R. Brown, *The Art of Preaching* (New York: Macmillan, 1924), p. 42.
4. Charles H. Spurgeon, *Lectures to My Students* (Grand Rapids: Zondervan, 1955), p. 72.
5. H. C. Brown, Jr., H. Gordon Clinard, and Jesse J. Northcutt, *Steps to the Sermon: A Plan for Sermon Preparation* (Nashville: Broadman, 1963), p. 137.
6. G. Ray Jordan, *You Can Preach* (Westwood, N.J.: Revell, 1951), p. 137.
7. Donald Macleod, *Here Is My Method* (Westwood, N.J.: Revell, 1952), p. 181.
8. H. C. Brown, Jr., *Southern Baptist Preaching* (Nashville: Broadman, 1959), pp. 112-13.
9. Brown, Clinard, and Northcutt, *Steps to the Sermon*, p. 68.
10. Ibid.
11. Ibid.
12. Ibid.

BIBLIOGRAPHY

* Braga, James. *How to Study the Bible.* Portland: Multnomah, 1982.

Fuller, Reginald H. *The Use of the Bible in Preaching.* Philadelphia: Fortress, 1981.

Henrichsen, Walter A. *A Layman's Guide to Interpreting the Bible.* Grand Rapids: Zondervan, 1976.

Hudson, D. F. *Teach Yourself New Testament Greek.* New York: Association, 1960.

Job, John B., ed. *How to Study the Bible.* Downers Grove, Ill.: InterVarsity, 1972.

Osborne, Grant R., and Stephen B. Woodward. *Handbook for Bible Study.* Grand Rapids: Baker, 1979.

* Perry, Lloyd M., and Robert D. Culver. *How to Search the Scriptures.* Grand Rapids: Baker, 1967.

Pitt-watson, Ian. *Preaching: A Kind of Folly.* Philadelphia: Westminster, 1976.

Randolph, David James. *The Renewal of Preaching.* Philadelphia: Fortress, 1969.

* Robertson, A. T. *The Minister and His Greek New Testament.* Grand Rapids: Baker, 1977.

Sproul, R. C. *Knowing Scripture.* Downers Grove, Ill.: InterVarsity, 1977.

Thompson, William D. *Preaching Biblically: Eisegesis and Interpretation.* Nashville: Abingdon; Abingdon Preacher's Library, 1981.

Wagner, Don M. *The Expository Method of G. Campbell Morgan.* Westwood, N.J.: Revell, 1957.

3

BIBLICAL PREACHING AND LOGICAL ORGANIZATION

> Ideally every minister ought to know something about homiletics and more about the art of preaching, but he should think most of all about the sermon. He ought to look upon himself not as a scientist with a lot of knowledge, or an artist with a gift of appreciation, but as a preacher with an ability to prepare all sorts of sermons. In order to do such work again and again, he ought to study the sermons of other men and then form habits all his own. (Andrew W. Blackwood, *The Preparation of Sermons* [Nashville: Abingdon, 1948], p. 20)

EXPOSITORY FOUNDATIONS FOR PROPOSITIONAL PREACHING

A good biblical sermon demands biblical exposition as a foundation. It must also include practical application for the listeners. These two factors are joined within a sermon into a logical framework. Preaching is the art of sermon presentation, whereas homiletics is the science of sermon construction. This science involves the systematic arrangement of the sermonic truths so that the listeners may experience what the Bible refers to as a "new birth" and then grow in spiritual maturity. This science of homiletics did not originate in theoretical dissertations but in general experience and observations.

Competent and discerning individuals have analyzed great preaching to discover what makes the sermons effective. They have noted the peculiarities of structure, content, and style that gave special forcefulness. Homiletics consists of the recorded result of this investigation, which can be useful for the training of preachers.

The first preachers of the gospel did not follow the rules of scientific sermon construction that we now consider essential to the highest effectiveness of pulpit discourse. Their sermons were more didactic than rhetorical in form and substance. In the founding of

Christianity, instruction was the principal object to be accomplished by preaching.

The earliest writers on homiletics, and the only contributors to the literature of this science among the early church Fathers were Chrysostom, "the golden-mouthed" preacher of Antioch and Constantinople, and Augustine of the Latin church.

Seven centuries passed after the time of Augustine without the production of any noteworthy treatise on the subject of homiletics. During the Scholastic period, extending from the latter part of the eleventh century to the middle of the fourteenth, attention was given once more to the subject of homiletics. The scholasticism of the twelfth and thirteenth centuries introduced into the construction of pulpit discourses a great number of rigid formalities such as minute divisions and subdivisions.

The essay of Monsieur Claude, a French Protestant divine who flourished in the latter part of the seventeenth century, marked the beginning of a new era in the development of sermonic science. Eminent preachers in the Roman Catholic and Protestant churches of France promoted pulpit eloquence with a new vigor. They seized the treasures of Grecian and Roman oratory and rendered them subservient to the work of the gospel ministry. An extended coverage of the correlation between rhetoric and homiletics can be found in *The Wycliffe Handbook of Preaching and Preachers*.[1] The rules of homiletics are intended not to bind but to guide the preacher in the construction of his sermons. The rules can give the preacher principles to start with and can forewarn him of possible perils. The preacher must work the theory into his own culture, so that he will execute it unconsciously. He can do this only in his own practice until it becomes second nature to him. This will take time. We learn how to live by living, and we learn how to preach by preaching. In neither living, nor preaching should we disregard the basic rules.

Henry Sloane Coffin (1877-1954), in his Warrack lectures of 1926, told the Scottish seminarians and divines to give increased attention to expository preaching, not just to teach the Bible "but to interpret life by the Bible."[2]

Origen (A.D. 184-254) has been credited with the expositional method most widely used today. Athanasius (A.D. 297-373) and Augustine (A.D. 354-430) were both informed in Origen's method of sermonizing, but Augustine's classic work *On Christian Doctrine* treats preaching style and offers an able expositor's method for handling biblical substance, which he discussed in books one, two, and three. Augustine's way of wedding words and Scripture teachings was exemplary and an evident mark of his interest and industry as well as "genius."

Our main concern should be that the sermon is biblical, logical, and practical. Arthur Allen states well the purpose for preaching: "The main purpose of preaching is to make the truth more clear and duty more urgent, to enlighten the mind, rouse the conscience, touch the heart, and persuade men and women to accept the gospel message and live the Christian life."[3]

THE DISCIPLINED APPROACH

Each day throughout his life Alexander Maclaren read one Bible chapter in Hebrew and another in Greek. He shut himself in his study every day of the week and devoted many exacting hours to the preparation of each sermon. Maclaren believed that if people wanted to hear him, they would come to Union Chapel in Manchester, England, where he was pastor for forty-five years and occasional preacher for six more years. He has been called the prince of expositors and the king of preachers.

Andrew W. Blackwood believes that Maclaren's preaching was mostly textual until he passed middle life, and that the shift to regular expository work came in his fifty-seventh year.[4] Most of Maclaren's sermons in *Expositions of Holy Scripture* seem to be textual at first glance, but closer examination shows that he always used his text in the light of the larger context, which actually made his handling expository.

THE CONTEXTUAL APPROACH

G. Campbell Morgan never handled any text, large or small, without closely relating it to its total context. Many people consider him the greatest of modern expository preachers. Wilbur M. Smith wrote, "For 40 years, beginning at the first decade of our century, the entire Christian world acknowledged that the greatest biblical expositor known in the pulpits of both England and America was Dr. G. Campbell Morgan."[5]

Before preaching from a book of the Bible, Morgan would read it through forty to fifty times. He would survey, condense, expand, and dissect it.

In his little book on preaching Morgan affirmed that truth, clarity, and passion were the essentials of a sermon. He claimed that getting the outline was the most important part of the homiletical process.

THE BALANCED APPROACH

Although Frederick W. Robertson died when he was only thirty-seven years old, A. W. Blackwood regards him "as the most influential preacher thus far in the English-speaking world."[6] In six years of expository work he covered only 1 and 2 Samuel, Acts, Genesis, and 1 and 2 Corinthians. Robertson died practically unknown outside his parish at Brighton, England, but his stature has continued to increase through his printed sermons.

THE IMAGINATIVE APPROACH

Joseph Parker is known especially for his *Parker's People's Bible,* twenty-seven volumes covering most of the Bible. This has been issued under the title *Preaching Through the Bible.* He said, "Of all the kinds of preaching, I love expository the most. You will understand this from the fact that during the last seven years I have expounded most of the first two books of the Pentateuch, the whole book of Nehemiah, the whole of Ecclesiastes, and nearly half of the Gospel of Matthew."[7]

Parker's sermons resemble the running commentary, biblical homilies with only fair evidence of an outline.

Essential Steps in Propositional Preaching

An effective biblical message should be marked by *logical organization.* Organization, or arranging the sermon for greater effectiveness, has been discussed by more than twenty men giving the Lyman Beecher Lectures on preaching at Yale University. They have expressed a diversity of opinion, but they are united in this: "The structure of the sermon may vary in many different ways, but the main point is that the sermon must have structure. It is true that only one or two of the hearers may recognize the presence or absence of structure for what it is; but they will all recognize the presence or absence of point, and point is the effect of structure."[8]

The wise expositor will recognize the advantage of working to a well-defined scheme. It will help him, and it will help his hearers. C. H. Spurgeon once confessed to his students:

> Ever since the day I was sent to a shop with a basket, and purchased a pound of rice, and on my way home saw a pack of hounds and felt it necessary to follow them over hedge and ditch (as I always did when I was a boy), and found when I reached home that all the goods were amalgamated—tea, mustard and rice—into one awful mess, I have understood the necessity of packaging up my subjects in good stout parcels, bound round with the thread of my discourse; and this makes me keep to firstly, secondly, and thirdly, however unfashionable that may now be. People will not drink your mustardly tea, nor will they enjoy muddled-up sermons, in which you cannot tell head and tail![9]

Following a systematic method of constructing a message does not rule out nor does it limit the guidance of the Holy Spirit. Orderliness, not confusion, is the evidence of the leading of the Holy Spirit. He still, even as at creation, brings order out of chaos. Several steps should be followed as one develops the propositional approach to a sermon.

DETERMINE THE SUBJECT

The subject is the one broad area that forms the basis of the sermon. It should be the summarizing core of the preaching portion. It represents the broad area out of which a number of themes might be chosen and from which one theme will be selected for the particular sermon at hand. The main thrust of the preaching portion must cover the major part of the passage. This will normally be discovered through induction. The sermonizer should be able to prove that the subject he determines for that particular portion is really the subject. This may sometimes be seen in the repetition of a core word.

When the preaching portion consists of one paragraph, the sermonizer should beware of selecting a main subject that has been mentioned in only one or two verses. The subject must cover the whole passage like a tent. If two or more paragraphs make up the preaching portion, he must beware lest the subject of just one paragraph is selected as the major one for the several paragraphs.

One of the best ways to determine the subject is to read the portion that is to serve as the basis for the sermon and then to ask, "What is the main center of attention for this whole passage?" Such a center of attention may be a doctrine to study; a duty to perform; a precept or maxim to explore; a problem to solve; or an occupation, profession, or calling to pursue. It will normally be one word.

Some general suggestions have been given regarding the process of obtaining subjects from various sources. There is a need for the cultivation of what is familiarly known as the "homiletic mind," a mind that is trained or that trains itself to make all resources, general as well as specific, tributary to the work of preaching. Subjects are obtained by acquisition, by reflection, and by exercise. If one is to gather sermonic subject material he must study diligently. He cannot read everything; therefore he must apply some limits in the area of his reading. The preacher must cultivate his memory. He must be careful to keep out of subject-matter ruts.

When the preacher has determined the subject of his preaching portion, which in turn is to be the subject of his sermon, he will be wise to gather information related to the subject. This process involves surveying the subject. The following ten questions will guide the sermonizer to material.

What have I read on the subject?
What have I observed that might throw light upon the subject?
What have I gleaned from the experience of the past on the subject?
What is the actual meaning of the subject?
What does the Scripture have to say on the subject?
What is my personal attitude or bias toward the subject?
What is the attitude or bias of my congregation toward the subject?
What famous quotations can I remember or locate pertaining to the subject?
What poetry can I recall which is related to the subject?
What is the real importance of the subject at this particular time?

FORMULATE THE THEME

The preaching portion has not only a subject but also a theme. The theme is the specific aspect of the subject being dealt with in that passage. It will circumscribe the subject by pointing out the boundaries of its discussion.

Each sermon has but one theme. It is the function of the theme to divide the subject and to suggest relationships. The theme will always be in the form of a phrase. It will be noted for brevity, clarity, and comprehensiveness of the main thrust of the sermon. The theme will indicate by its wording the sermonic purpose. This could be referred to as the direction of the sermonic purpose.

This direction may be why, how, when, or where as related to the subject. The sermon direction indicated at this point will establish the sermonic interrogative.

Subject	Theme	Sermon Direction and Interrogative
Prayer	The profit of prayer	Why
Intercessory prayer	The necessity for intercessory prayer	Why
God's work	Supporting God's work	Why or How
Praying	Effective praying	How
Tithing	The ability to tithe	How
Soul winner	How to become a soul winner	How
Discouragement	Overcoming discouragement	How

When the theme has been determined, the sermonizer should probe it in order to clarify its meaning and to collect information concerning it. The following ten questions will aid in this analyzation process.

What was there in the preaching portion that led you to select this particular theme?

Are there terms in the theme that should be defined? This may be a necessary step both for the preacher and for the anticipated listeners.

Are there similes and metaphors that would throw light upon the theme?

What is your personal relationship to this theme?

What relationship would your anticipated audience have to this theme?

What statements of Scripture prove or strengthen this theme?

What relationship exists between each segment within the preaching portion and the theme?

Is this theme suitable for the time, place, and occasion?

Are there technical terms in the theme? If so, they should be explained and put into nontechnical forms.

Are there words in the theme that are employed in an unusual way?

SELECT A TITLE

The title for a sermon is the announced or advertised form of the theme. The thought is the same but the title is phrased for bulletin board appeal. The title serves not only to attract the listeners but also provides a helpful device for filing sermons.

The title should be in keeping with the mood of the sermon, the character of the audience, and the nature of the occasion. It is not wise to have more than four thought-carrying words in the sermon title. Long titles tend to decrease rather than increase people's interest. Some themes may serve as good titles without any change in the wording. In other cases, a change of wording will tend to arouse more curiosity while still suggesting the actual content of the message.

The appealing title must not be confused with the cheap sensational title. Some examples of the latter are: "Charlie McCarthy or Jesus Christ," "Why Every Preacher Should Go to Hell," "A Nudist in a Graveyard," and "The Baptist Preacher Who Lost His Head at a Dance."

The emphatic word title. The most popular and prevalent title is that which employs the emphatic word in the phrase giving direction.

Title: "The Habit of Thankfulness"[10]
Text: 1 Thessalonians 5:18, "In everything give thanks . . . "

The interrogative sentence title.

Title: "How May We Know Jesus Better?"
Text: Philippians 3:10, "That I may know him . . ."

The imperative sentence title.

Title: "Be Born Again in Christ"
Text: John 3:5-7, "Unless one is born of water and the Spirit, he
   cannot enter into the Kingdom of God."

The declarative sentence title.

Title: "Life Is an Echo"
Text: Matthew 7:2, "By your standard of measure, it will be mea-
   sured to you."

The limiting word title. The phrase of direction is sometimes
established by adding modifiers or limiting words to the title.

Title: "The Second Mile"
Text: Matthew 5:41, "Whoever shall force you to go one mile, go
   with him two."

The title should be carefully worded in order to generate interest. It should suggest the subject but not "give it away" altogether.
It is extremely important that the title be honest. The audience
should feel that the title fits the message.

Make your sermon titles command attention, stir the imagination, and create a desire within the prospective attendant to hear
what you have to say.

As a stimulus to the reader, a large number of sermon titles are
listed in the Appendix: Sermon Ideas for a Year in the Word.

CORRELATE THE ELEMENTS

The *subject* tells what the sermon is about. The *theme* indicates
that particular aspect of the subject that will be most useful for presentation to the people. The *title* gives the final phrasing of the theme
as it goes into the bulletin, the newspaper, and on the bulletin board.
It covers the same idea as the theme but may be worked quite differ-
ently to make it interesting and attractive. It is best not to use the
word *topic* because it is often used identically with *theme*, *title*, and
subject.

The process of limiting a subject through the use of themes will be seen as we take the subject of prayer and list some of the possible themes that can be drawn from it.

The necessity of prayer	Answers to prayer
The value of prayer	Intercessory prayer
The time for prayer	Family prayer
The power of prayer	Hindrance to prayer
The purpose of prayer	Practical prayer
The methods of prayer	Attitudes in prayer
The results of prayer	Places to pray
The conditions of prayer	Worship through prayer
The problems of prayer	Posture of prayer
Praying in the Spirit	The privilege of prayer
Perseverance in prayer	Faith and prayer
The preeminence of prayer	The scope of prayer

The more specific the theme, so long as it is important, the more suggestive it will be and the easier it will be to handle.

CONSTRUCT A PROPOSITION

Importance of propositions. The proposition occupies the focal point in the sermon outline. The term *proposition* is used in its technical sense as being a sentence that by means of the copula verb affirms or denies some predicate or some subject. This part (of which there is only one) of the sermon has been referred to by different writers as the central idea, the controlling assertion, the statement, the big truth, the subject sentence, and the thesis. It is this sentence that is the integrating center of the sermon.

The proposition's importance is furthermore noted as being likened to the example of a tree, in which the argument forms the branches, the proposition the trunk, and the text the root. So the proposition adds strength and beauty to the discourse. It promotes stability of structure, unity of thought, and forcefulness of impact. No sermon is ready for preaching, or for writing, until one can express its theme in a short, pregnant sentence, as clear as crystal. Jowett is reported to have said that getting that sentence was the hardest, most exacting, and most fruitful labor in his study.

Characteristics of propositions. Austin Phelps, perhaps the outstanding champion of the proposition, in his notable work, *The Theory of Preaching,* 1881, devoted eighty-two pages to this part of the sermon. The proposition is that part of the discourse by which the subject is defined. A proposition is a promise.

A common sentence form used for the proposition is the simple *declaration*, which might be called the declarative proposition. It is a clear, concise statement of the theme in declarative form. It also may be given in two other forms—the *interrogation* and the *exhortation*.

Every word should be essential to the proposition's meaning. Ordinarily a good proposition is stated in no more than eight to fifteen words. Its special function is to promote stability of thought so that it will be applicable both in Bible times and at present. The propositional sentence is never compound in form. Although it appears at a specific point on the sermon outline, it may be given in oral presentation at different points as the sermon is delivered.

The proposition will be characterized by unity in that it will have but one subject, seek but one aim, and make but one lasting impression. It should be expressed in a single sentence, with the simplest possible syntax and in the most definite terms. Every word and every connection of the words in this statement must be pondered with care, since the proposition should be complete. Its simplicity may be nullified through the inclusion of words that are unintelligible or of doubtful meaning to the hearers. It is therefore necessary to exclude technical terms and figurative language.

The proposition will be marked by accuracy in that it will be carefully worded so that it will conform to the truth. Its clarity will be evident as it makes clear the aim of the sermon. It should be expressed in as few words as possible. Since it is characterized by universality, only proper names pertaining to deity should be used within it. The preacher should be certain that the proposition is worthy of demanding the time of the congregation for consideration.

Great preaching is always in the present tense. It must speak to the concerns of the day in the thought forms and language of the day. It is important, therefore, that this propositional sentence be true to the impact of Scripture and also that it be relevant to human experience. The proposition must be stated in the form of a timeless truth that was valid for Bible times and is still valid for the day in which it is being preached.

A good proposition should be characterized by human interest. To create human interest the proposition should be personal in the sense that it touches the mood and manner of speech of those who will see or hear it. It should be in touch with life as people live it. It should touch the basic and fundamental questions that men and women ask, and it should relate to the basic experiences of life.

Kinds of propositions.

A statement of *evaluation* or *judgment.* Example: Praying is profitable.

A statement of *obligation* or *duty.* Example: It is necessary for Christians to engage in intercessory prayer. Christians should support God's work.

A statement of *activity* or *potentiality* (the emphasis is upon ability). Example: We can become more effective in praying. Every Christian can tithe. A Christian can overcome discouragement.

Forms of propositions. It is important that the substance of the proposition be recognized and clearly understood by the listener. The preacher should repeat it until he is certain it has been grasped by the listener. This repetition may become less monotonous when the form of the proposition is varied.

The declarative form: "Prayer brings many benefits."
The interrogative form: "What are the benefits of prayer?"
The hortatory form: "Keep seeking the benefits of prayer!"
The exclamatory form: "Think of the many benefits of prayer."

Phrasing for propositions. The method of introducing the proposition may be varied by using one of the following phrases.

"I invite your attention . . ."
"The text contains . . ."
"This discourse will be devoted to . . ."
"I propose to speak . . ."
"I aim to prove . . ."
"My intention is to illustrate . . ."
"The text is an example of . . . "
"The service of this hour will consider . . ."
"Let us consider this truth . . ."
"Our common experience emphasizes . . ."

In the sermon outline the proposition appears just following the introduction. In normal presentation it is delivered at this same point in the sermon. There are times, however, when the place of presentation of the proposition can be varied. The main points of the sermon can be presented and then the proposition delivered, which will then serve to provide a unifying thought climax to the sermon. This is the difference between deductive and inductive sermon presentation.

FOCUS ON TRANSITIONS

Meaning of transitions. A transitional sentence is a rhetorical bridge between the core of the sermon (the proposition) and the development of the sermon (the body). This rhetorical bridge is a transitional sentence that gathers what has preceded it in the sermon and makes the logical transition to what follows.

Components of transitions. The transitional sentence is a connective composed of the proposition, a key word, and an interrogative or interrogative substitute.

Interrogatives in transitions. An interrogative substitute is sometimes used in place of a simple interrogative in order that the sentence structure of the transition may be enhanced. When the construction of the transitional sentence demands the use of an interrogative substitute in place of an interrogative, there are three that may be used. "Because of" may be substituted for "why." "By" plus a verbal may be substituted for "how." "In which" or "at which" may be substituted for "where."

1. Selecting interrogatives. How does the sermonizer know which interrogative to select? The sermonizer looks at the proposition he has just established and determines which of the following six questions this sermon should answer for the listener.

How can I . . . ?   Where should I . . . ?
Why should I . . . ?   Where can I . . . ?
When should I . . . ?   Why is it . . . ?

The interrogative adverb from one of the preceding questions is now taken as the sermonic interrogative. This sermonic interrogative or its substitute will be used in the transitional sentence.

The interrogative or interrogative substitute is followed in the transitional sentence by a key word. This is always a plural noun that will characterize the main points of the message. The kind of key word to be used is determined by placing the sermonic interrogative in front of the proposition and thus forming a sermonic interrogation.

2. Constructing interrogatives. A sermonic interrogation is made up of the proposition preceded by one of four interrogative words: *why, how, when,* and *where.* This interrogation is a tool that leads to a key word. Since the sermonic interrogation is only a tool of construction, it does not appear on the written sermon outline but may be given in delivery several times during the course of the sermon. The sermonizer then selects a plural noun that will provide a logical answer to the question he has just asked. There is only one key word in a sermon.

3. Testing interrogatives. The sermonizer must test the contents of the preaching portion to discover which interrogative is most prominent. This involves discovering whether or not certain key phrases summarize the subject of the passage. The following lists may serve as guides but are not exhaustive.

If the passage calls for support or acceptance of its subject because of one of the following key phrases, then the sermon will have the interrogative adverb *why* as its center. Each key phrase includes a key word (a noun in the plural that will characterize the main points of the sermon).

Arguments set forth
Benefits to be derived
Bequests promised
Blessing to be received
Commands given
Dangers thereby avoided
Effects produced
Gains to be received
Guarantees provided
Honors to be bestowed
Imperatives given
Improvements to be made
Incentives offered
Injunctions set forth
Invitations extended
Issues at stake

Joys to be realized
Judgments to be rendered
Lessons that can be learned
Losses sustained
Needs manifested
Obligations placed upon us
Orders given
Penalties inflicted
Predictions made
Privileges offered
Profits to be gained
Reasons set forth
Results to be obtained
Rewards promised
Satisfaction to be gained
Values to be realized

If the passage provides support of its subject as indicated by one of the following key phrases, each beginning with *by*, then the sermon will have the interrogative adverb *how* as its center.

Avoiding blunders
Avoiding dangers
Avoiding excesses
Avoiding extremes
Avoiding the mistakes of
Following instructions
Following guides
Following methods
Following the patterns of
Following the plans of
Following the practices of
Following prescriptions
Following the rules of
Following the steps of
Following the stipulations
Heeding the commands of
Heeding the laws of
Heeding the precautions of

Heeding the sayings of
Making adequate preparations
Making use of the provision of
Mastering details
Not giving way to one's fears
Obeying directives
Obeying injunctions
Obeying the teachers
Observing principles
Overcoming barriers
Practicing the fundamentals of
Practicing the lessons of
Surmounting obstacles
Taking advantage of the means
    provided
Taking advantage of the power of
Taking the better alternatives
Working within the system

If the passage provides support of its subject by providing a series of times, then the sermon will have the interrogative *when* as its center. The key word or phrase may be seasons of the year, times of the day, months of the year, or periods in life.

If the passage provides support of its subject by providing a series of area indications, then the sermon will have the interrogative *where* as its center. The key word may be areas, groups, places, locations, positions, meetings, or regions.

Integrating the transitions. It will be helpful at this point to study a series of examples that combine a proposition and a corresponding transitional sentence:

> Proposition: Every Christian should pray.
> (Sermonic Interrogation: Why should every Christian pray?)
> Transitional Sentence: Because of the blessings to be gained, every Christian should pray.

> Proposition: Every Christian can be effective in prayer.
> (Sermonic Interrogation: How can every Christian be effective in prayer?)
> Transitional Sentence: By following the instructions in Matthew 6:5-15, every Christian can be effective in prayer.

> Proposition: Every Christian should pray.
> (Sermonic Interrogation: Where should Christians pray?)
> Transitional Sentence: There are several places in which every Christian should pray.

ESTABLISH MAIN POINTS

The main body of the sermon lying between the introduction and the conclusion is an opening up of the theme, with an analysis for its framework, and containing illustration and application. The body of the sermon expounds the text, develops the proposition, or presents the argument.

Unity of main points. There is a close correlation between the key word of the sermon and the main points. The main points should correspond to the key word. If the key word is *reasons*, then each main point of the sermon will be a *reason* why the proposition should be accepted.

Derivation of main points. When preaching on one portion of Scripture, all the main points should be taken from that passage. Each point will be clearly marked by its scriptural undergirding, which consists of listing after each point the Scripture reference and a quotation from that reference that supports the main point. The following is an example.

> Text: Deuteronomy 6:5-13
>   I. Remember God. V. 12: "Then watch yourself, lest you forget the Lord."

II. Love God. V. 5: "And you shall love the Lord thy God."
III. Declare God. Vv. 6-7a: "And these words which I am commanding you today shall be on your heart; and you shall teach them diligently."
IV. Serve God. V. 13: "You shall fear only the Lord your God; and you shall worship Him."

Characteristics of main points. Certain mechanical rules of grammar and structure should be observed. The main points should be parallel to one another in form as far as possible. This will aid the memory of the preacher and the people listening. The points should be clearly underlined, thus aiding the visual memory of the preacher. If he preaches with notes, such underlining will aid him in spotting the main points at a glance.

Each point should contain only one idea. This will mean that the preacher will avoid the word *and* in the statement of the points. In order that the main points may be clear in meaning to the listener, figurative language should be avoided. It is not necessary to arrange the points in the order in which they occur within the Bible passage. They should be arranged in respect to the purpose that the preacher desires to accomplish.

In summary, the main points of a sermon should be:

Few in number
Mutually exclusive
Clear
Comprehensive of the
    content of proposition
In similar relationship to
    the subject
Forceful in logic

Vitally related to the
    proposition
Similar to one another in form
Well proportioned
Progressive in movement
Tied in with the text
Concise

Ordering of main points. There are ten general focal points around which the sermonizer can order his main points.

Chronological: when we arrange the points in time order, as in narrating events.
Geographical: when the points are arranged according to an orderly directional sequence, such as from east to west or north to south.
Quantitative: when the main points refer to items of differing sizes or amounts from small to large or vice versa.
Deductive: proceeding in main points from a general truth to specific instances.
Inductive: when the main points take us from specific cases to the general truth they teach.

Psychological: such as Alan Monroe's motivated sequence. One may choose to follow the five-step outline in persuasive speeches. He says we first take the *attention step,* making the audience wish to listen; then the *need step,* creating the idea that this is the thing to do, believe, or feel to satisfy the need; then the *satisfaction step,* which seeks to get the audience to agree that your proposal is correct; then comes the *visualization step,* when we cause the listener to picture himself enjoying the satisfaction of doing, believing, or feeling this action; and, finally comes the *action step,* when we ask the hearer to do, believe, accept, or feel what we present.

Cause and effect (or vice versa): when we proceed from a cause to its effects, or from the effects to the cause.

Negation: when we show that a thing is not this, not that, nor the other. The positive answer is given in the conclusion.

Partitional: when we divide anything into its consituent or logical parts.

Problem solving: when we lay down a problem and suggest various solutions to it, all leading us up to the final and best one.

Number of main points. The number of main points in a message will be controlled by the content of the preaching portion. There should not be less than two points and normally not more than five. The average listener cannot remember more than five points. Topical messages will often follow special plans.

SUBDIVIDE MAIN POINTS

Meaning of subdivisions. Amplification is the process of using subdivisions that will amplify and explain the main points of the message. There will be at least two and normally not more than five of these under each main point.

Characteristics of subdivisions. At least one in the series will always be one of application to the immediate congregation. This assures direct practical contact between the sermon and the listener at regular intervals during the sermon rather than waiting for all of the application to appear toward the close of the message.

Since it is desired that these subdivisions be remembered by the listener, it is important that they be short in form, few in number, and similar in form. As many of the subdivisions as possible should be drawn from the passage upon which the sermonizer is basing his message. Parallelism in form will aid memorization of the subpoint even as it does the main points. As with the main points, only numbers would be used to indicate the points. We avoid using letters both when formulating and when recalling an outline.

The subpoint does not need to be stated in complete sentence form, but it should be specific enough and complete enough so that the content may be readily recalled.

Forms of subdivisions. Some of the forms or modes of development are the illustrative, the persuasive, the analytic, and the didactic.

Illustrative development. This mode aims to instruct the hearer by unfolding to him divine truth as illustrated by character. Such a development promotes vivacity of style and aids the preacher in setting forth a great variety of truth in an attractive and impressive form. It also promotes permanence of impression and thus aids the hearer in embodying the truth in his life.

Persuasive development. This mode aims at moving the will of the hearer. It imposes on the preacher himself the same duties he inculcates on others. It directly impresses upon the hearer the motives underlying a Christian life. In this kind of development he will take notice of possible excuses, will deal with these at the outset of a discourse, and then will proceed to enforce the duty.

Analytic development. This is the favorite of logical minds. It is the one to be used when one's purpose is instruction.

Didactic development. There is danger in using the didactic process of development in that preaching may degenerate into a barren intellectualism. However, true didactic preaching, with sound thinking put in concrete popular form, will avoid the extremes of intellectualism on the one side and sentimentalism or sensationalism on the other.

Processes in subdivisions. There are at least six processes that may be used in developing an idea as set forth in a main point of a sermon. These processes may be intermingled according to the leading of the preacher, the demands of logic, and the limitations of the passage of Scripture.

1. Development by interrogation. There are six interrogative words that will help to unlock the meaning of most main points. These six words are *how, why, when, where, who,* and *what.* Apply these words one by one to the main point and answer the question thus formed in the subpoint. One of these interrogative words will often give more than one subpoint. This is the easiest and most often used process of development.

2. Development by exposition. One means of exposition is that of definition. A definition may be called good when it renders the idea clearer than it was before the definition was given. It should present nothing more or less than is contained in the idea. In formulating definitions one should avoid too great formality and subtlety. We may define by giving synonyms, which are words having the same or nearly the same meaning.

The homiletician may seek to define by classification chronologically, scholastically, financially, affiliatively, positionally, and so forth. He may choose to study the root meaning of the words involved in the main point and thus define by etymology. By telling what the main point is not, he will define by negation. Defining by context is the process of identifying the object in its surroundings. If one sets forth a series of instances or examples, whether real or hypothetical, he can define by illustration.

The process of exposition may involve telling or presenting a series of events in a story form, using the following four steps: establish the setting and get the action started; develop the main body of the incident; bring the incident to its logical climax; draw the conclusion that may well be a logical application for the listener. This is exposition by narration. When we put into word-picture form persons and objects, thus telling how persons or things look, feel, or act, we are using description as a means of exposition.

3. Development by argumentation. Argumentation may be defined as the art or activity by which the preacher seeks to draw a response from his listeners by reasoned discourse. It involves the defense of some element within the main point.

Inductive reasoning is the logical process used to obtain a proposition. It consists of drawing inferences from facts, experience, and evidence. It is a process of reasoning from a part to a whole, from particulars to generals, from individuals to universals. Inductive reasoning is expressed in two kinds of argument. The first is argument from example.

The second kind of argument is that of analogy. In this, the ground of inference is resemblance between two individual objects or kinds of objects. The inference is that they resemble one another in some point known to belong to the one but not known to belong to the other.

Deductive reasoning applies a generalization to a specific case. Every deductive argument contains two premises and a conclusion. Deductive argument is expressed in two kinds of argument. The first is argument from cause. Such an argument assumes that a prescribed set of conditions will bring about a prescribed set of effects. Argument from sign is one that gives an indication that the point is true without trying to explain why it is true.

4. Development by persuasion. Some of the points of the motivated sequence as set forth by Alan Monroe might be used as subpoints with a view toward moving the will of the listener. These include the attention step, the need step, the satisfaction step, the visualization step, and the action step.

5. Development by thought categorization. This process of development makes use of some of the common patterns of thinking as bases for subpoints. Among the general categories that might

be applied as a guide in the homiletical development of an idea are the following:

> If the main point involves a person, this person may be sketched as to heredity, environment, development, capacity, character, career, achievement, and reputation.
>
> If the main point is an event, this may be examined with regard to time, place, antecedents, consequences, human participation, and evidences of divine providence.
>
> If the main point involves relationships, these relations may be itemized as being in relation to self, neighbor, and God.
>
> The time order may be applied to the main point showing its relation to the past, present, and future.
>
> The category of source, nature, and effect may be used.
>
> If one is considering a biblical miracle of healing, he may survey the case, cause, cure, and consequences.
>
> The category of size or dimensions involves breadth, length, depth, and height.
>
> The category of social relationships involves husbands and wives, children and parents, servants and masters.
>
> The category of spiritual status includes saints and sinners, pre-conversion and post-conversion, conduct and compensation.
>
> The spiritual development category might include the call, commission, conduct, and compensation.

6. Development by exegesis of the scriptural undergirding. The scriptural undergirding of a main point in a message includes the Bible reference that serves as the basis for the point. The portion of the verse that specifically sets forth the truth of the main point is given as a direct quotation from Scripture. The homiletician may select words and phrases within this scriptural undergirding that need definition and amplification. Each subpoint will have one of the segments of the undergirding Scripture verse as its core.

FORMULATE AN INTRODUCTION

Meaning of introductions. Introductions to sermons are sometimes called "the crosses of preachers," because beginnings are always difficult. The introduction clarifies the reason this audience should listen to this preacher discuss this subject on this occasion. The preacher should prepare the introduction so that it establishes an interrelationship connecting text, theme, speaker, audience, and occasion.

The introduction serves to make a transition or bridge from the secular to the spiritual. It meets members of the congregation where they are in daily living, and then the sermon proceeds to lead them gradually to the foot of the cross for salvation, sanctification, or service.

Characteristics of introductions. To fulfill its function the introduction must be relatively brief and interesting; it must arouse but not retain the hearer's attention; it must be simple and not itself require explanation; it must be relevant but not highly controversial.

A good introduction will do more than introduce the preacher and the subject, and give the setting of the message. It will prepare the minds of the congregation for the reception and digestion of the sermon. It will attract the attention of the audience and arouse their interest.

The introduction should contain nothing foreign to the purpose of the discourse. An introduction should be: brief, pertinent, clear, in harmony with the subject, appropriate to the sermon, natural, direct, friendly, adjusted to the mental state of the audience, well planned.

An introduction should *not* include: flattery, apologies, triteness, complexity, abstractness, technicality, dry details about the background of the text, too much revelation of what is to follow, irrelevant humor, or verbosity.

Construction of introductions. Though spoken first, the introduction is made near the last. Since the function of an introduction is to lead into something, the point to which the hearers are to be led must be determined first. Making the introduction last will protect the preacher from the subtle temptation of having too long an introduction. Therefore the introduction should not be written until the rough draft of the body and conclusion has been finished.

The introduction is composed of an introductory approach sentence, an outlined section, and a biblical orientation.

In formulating the approach sentence, the sermonizer should select a word or idea within the proposition that needs definition, clarification, or amplification. This word or idea will become the core of the introduction. This core thought of the introduction should be developed in terms of where the listeners are in daily living. The sermon thus begins with a secular discussion of the word or phrase selected from the proposition.

The outlined section of the introduction will consist of a development of the approach sentence. It should be kept in mind that the introduction is designed to point the listeners to the truth to be developed within the sermon.

The biblical orientation is inserted within the sermon outline as the final segment of the introduction. It is the sermonic bridge between the secular segments of the introduction and the body of the sermon. This explanation will put the sermon into its biblical context. It will involve drawing certain relevant material from the Bible study itself, which material will be helpful to the listeners. The explanation will also include any unique features of the kind of sermon being presented. This will help to prepare the listener to follow its development. The following is an example.

Introduction: Prosperity has its price. (Approach Sentence)
1. Prosperity: "A thriving condition, good fortune, success."
2. "Watch lest prosperity destroy generosity" (H. W. Beecher).
Biblical Orientation:
1. (Show that the subject and theme of the sermon are inherent within the preaching portion.)
2. (Point out features of the content and context of the preaching portion that may have interest value as far as the theme is concerned.)

Delivery of introductions. In Germany it is common, but not universal, to give the introduction before the text. In England, and in our own country, it is the practice to put it after the text.

The time used by the introduction should occupy no more than fifteen percent of the speaking time. The introduction is only the porch the listener must cross in order to get into the main house. The preacher should not keep his people waiting on the porch but should usher them into the house as soon as is convenient.

Purposes of introductions. The preacher may select one or more purposes from the following list and thereby vary the content of the introduction.

To establish contact with the audience
To arouse interest in the text or theme being discussed by emphasizing its importance and clarifying the terms
To remove prejudice against the speaker or subject
To show the pertinence of the theme to the occasion
To bring calmness to the audience
To enlighten the listeners regarding the background of the message
To point out the necessity for finding a solution to a particular problem

To clarify the unique features of form and content that the sermon will possess

To adjust the message to the occasion by making the theme relevant

To secure attention

To lead the thoughts of the hearers gracefully to the subject

To create favorable regard for the subject

To secure the good will of the audience

To prepare the audience for the message

To exhibit the text in its connections

To prepare the mind of the hearers to receive the truth

To show the importance of the subject

To stimulate inquiry

To refer to relevant matters of great local, national, and international interest

To stir curiosity

Variety in introductions. There are many items that one may use in the process of writing an introduction. One or more of these (in the list below) may be used as part of the approach sentence or as part of the outlined content that follows.

A startling statement

A challenging question or series of questions

A pertinent quotation

A witty, humorous, or amusing incident

An epigram (a bright or witty thought tersely and ingeniously expressed)

A vivid word picture

A definition

A comparison

A discovery

A correction

A concession

A paradox (an assertion seemingly contradictory, or opposed to common sense, yet are in fact

A rhetorical question (a question not intended to elicit an answer, but inserted for rhetorical effect)

A statement of a problem

A proposal

A personal observation

A commendation

A statement of the special importance of the theme

A conundrum (a puzzling question of which the answer is a pun or involves a pun or a riddle)

A prediction or prophecy

A brief poem

A brief history of the theme

A proverb

A prayer

A pertinent, courteous reference to a previous speaker

A reference to a current event

An incident from pastoral experience

A reference to a current event

An incident from pastoral experience

A reference to a special season

A reference to a cartoon	A sentence from a widely
An object lesson (if speaking to a "believing" audience)	read book
	A comparison with other Scripture
An announcement of something significant	A concrete example or illustration
A dramatic description	

Suggestions for introductions. Get the audience into one closely knit group located in the same section of the auditorium. This is known as polarizing the audience.

If possible, be alone on the platform, thus creating one center of attention.

From a persuasion standpoint, see that the lighting is adequate for both speaker and audience. Have a concentration of light on the speaker.

Avoid too high a platform. Failure to observe this will cause drowsiness on the part of the hearers.

If the speaker is introduced, let the introduction be short and to the point.

Walk to the pulpit with quiet confidence and assurance.

Establish physical directness by looking at the people rather than at the physical features of the room.

See that the temperature of the room is adjusted not to rise above or go below 68 degrees during the service, else the audience will become uncomfortable.

Have proper ventilating arrangements made before speaking, in order to keep the audience comfortable and supplied with fresh air.

Avoid distracting mannerisms such as fumbling with a watch, adjusting the pulpit lamp, removing hymn books from the pulpit, or rearranging your Bible.

Guard against an overuse of gestures in the introduction. Give the impression that you have a reserve of power for the climax of the sermon.

DETERMINE THE CONCLUSION

Importance of conclusions. If a safe landing is the most important part of an airplane trip, the harvest the most important part of farming, the concluding chapter the most important part of a book, we may also say that the conclusion is the most important part of a sermon.

The best orators, both secular and religious, of ancient and modern times have regarded the proper conclusion of a discourse as of the highest importance.

The importance of the conclusion is not only that it makes the last impression of the sermon on the congregation but also that it is the summing up and gathering together of all parts of the sermon for practical effect.

Preachers seldom neglect to prepare an introduction to a sermon, but very often neglect to provide a conclusion; yet the latter is even more important than the former.

Functions of conclusions. The conclusion corresponds to the introduction because, like the introduction, it takes into account the hearer's mental and emotional states. The problem of the one is to win interest for the discussion, and of the other to utilize such interest after it has been won.

The conclusion accentuates the practical significance of the sermon. It discloses the moral earnestness of the preacher and accentuates the rhetorical completeness of the sermon. It is that part of the discourse in which the discussion is drawn to a close and the truth fitted to life.

Nature of conclusions. The conclusion should be so formulated that it will aim at practical effect. It should be presented with a warmth that appeals to the heart. The preacher should employ his inventive powers to insert analogies between abstract truth and facts of every kind.

The word *conclusion* has two meanings: "to come to an end," and "to bring the mind to a decision." The conclusion of a sermon, therefore, refers not only to its closing sentences, but especially to its application to the congregation so as to produce in them the intended result.

There are two parts to a conclusion. The first of these is the objective sentence, which is the first sentence of the conclusion. It is formulated by beginning with "Therefore, we (the ones to whom the message is addressed) should." This will be followed by the response anticipated or desired by the speaker. This response will consist of a combination of the proposition of the sermon and the purpose behind the presentation of the message.

In some cases, this objective sentence will be similar in form to the proposition. This is especially true when a proposition of obligation is used. The objective sentence will always begin with "therefore" and will always include "should."

Characteristics of conclusions. Whatever be the character of the sermon, a fitting conclusion may be made to it by seizing upon some thought or incident that gathers into itself the general thought of the whole discourse, so as to present it as a unit in a new and impressive form.

Such expressions as "in conclusion," "finally," and "one word more," are not only unnecessary but also focus attention on the imminent close of the sermon. For many listeners this diversion of attention torpedoes the life-impact of the sermon's message.

The following are characteristics of good conclusions: brevity, clarity, correct phrasing, intensity, freshness, variety, well-prepared content, vigor, climax, practicality, appropriateness, naturalness, personal application, positiveness, distinctiveness, impressiveness, persuasiveness, effectiveness, strikingness, eloquence.

The charm that lies in genuine oratory is not for an age but for all time. Study the conclusions of Jean Baptiste Massillon and the other great French preachers of the seventeenth century, of Robert Hall and Thomas Chalmers, of Henry Melville and John Caird. Without any ambitious or artificial straining after effect, the conclusion should be based on the thrust of the sermon.

Kinds of conclusions. Beyond the objective sentence, one of these kinds of conclusions may be added.

1. The recapitulation conclusion. This is the formal summary, in which the main points are repeated without changing their terminology; the paraphrased summary, in which the main points are repeated in words arousing new interest; the common sense summary, in which the main points are rephrased in ordinary words; the epigrammatic summary, in which the main points are reduced to a single word for each point (for example, *stop, look, listen*).

2. The application conclusion. This kind suggests ways and means of carrying out the suggestions made in the sermon. The application is focalized sharply on the daily life.

3. The motivation conclusion. This appeals to some lofty motive. It has been suggested by Charles Koller that there are seven basic appeals to the heart: the appeal to altruism, aspiration, curiosity, duty, fear, love, and reason. (An extensive discussion of these appeals can be found in Koller's book *Expository Preaching Without Notes.*)

4. The contrast conclusion. This kind of conclusion presents a direct contrast in thought and mood from that set forth in the sermon. An example setting forth the need for this kind of conclusion can be seen when the body of the sermon has emphasized the negative. The conclusion in that case should present a positive approach thus ending the message on a positive note.

5. The anticipatory conclusion. This erects "straw men" (anticipated objections) and proceeds to destroy them.

Procedures for conclusions. There are numerous errors to avoid in conclusions.

> Avoid letting interest lag in the conclusion. Hold sufficient material and force in reserve to make the conclusion an effective climax.

Avoid making the conclusion too long. If the conclusion is long,

the interest will tend to lag. The conclusion, like the introduction, varies in length according to the length of the entire
sermon. As a general rule the conclusion should be brief,
consuming no more than ten percent of the total time of
delivery.

Avoid giving the impression that you are about to conclude
when you are not.

Avoid introducing new material, especially if it is not pertinent
to the theme.

Avoid concluding a serious message with a joke or humorous
remark. The use of such humor in the conclusion will likely
destroy the spiritual thrust of the message.

Avoid monotony in conclusions.

Avoid trite, hackneyed conclusions.

Avoid apologizing in conclusions.

Avoid a formal announcement of your conclusions.

The use of personal pronouns (especially you, your, yours, we,
us, and ours) gives the message a direct, warm, personal touch.

If the main points of the message have been stated as nega-
tives, the preacher should then employ a positive conclusion. The
message should be ended on a positive note.

Options in conclusions. The speaker should vary the instru-
ments used in formulating conclusions, as suggested by the options
in the following list.

A restatement of the text	An apt quotation
A fitting poem	An earnest exhortation
A story or illustration	An appeal to the imagination
A contrasting truth	A prayer
An answer to objections	A call for public response
A challenge	A dare
A rhetorical question	An appreciation
A proverb	A promise
A suggestion of ways and means	A striking statement
A parable	A hymn

One of the most familiar forms of conclusions is a prayer in
which the appeal for decision is cast into a brief petition for divine
aid in carrying it out.

Moods in conclusions. The changing of the mood in presenting
conclusions provides a means for gaining variety. The nature of the
sermon, the content, and the occasion will provide guidance in the
mood for the conclusion.

The quiet mood
The contemplative mood
The mood of overwhelming appeal
The joyful mood
The comforting mood
The worshipful (devotional) mood

TWO VARIATIONS IN PROPOSITIONAL PREACHING

TOPICAL PREACHING

The traditional approach.
1. Reservations about the traditional approach. A topical sermon is one that is confined to the discussion of a single leading idea. Very often the theme, which is especially prominent, is selected first, and then comes the text. These are sometimes called *subject sermons* because the divisions are obtained from the subject and not from the text. It is easy for this kind of message to become only a religious address rather than a sermon.

A topical discussion that is not at the same time an exposition of Scripture is not really a sermon. The subject of a topical sermon should be the subject of the passage upon which it is based. This subject must be developed in such a way that it sets forth the true meaning of the passage, understood in the light of the historical and exegetical study. Then and only then is it truly a topical sermon. Such a sermon will in its own way be an exposition of Scripture. This is one reason for many of our British homileticians referring only to biblical sermons rather than to topical, textual, and expository messages.

2. Advantages of the traditional approach. The topical sermon has been considered as the most oratorical species of pulpit address. It lends itself to unity of discussion and power of impression because it embraces a single idea that can be expressed in a terse proposition.

T. Harwood Pattison notes that the apostles often preached on topics without texts. Chrysostom, Augustine, and other church Fathers did the same. This kind of preaching was almost universally the method used by the great French preachers.

It lends itself to rhetorical perfection. The preacher is encouraged to make a more thorough examination of the subject. Jonathan Edwards exemplified this in his preaching. This kind of sermon trains the mind of the preacher to develop a breadth of view of a subject.

3. Weaknesses of the traditional approach. The traditional approach to topical preaching has some weaknesses. The number

of broad subjects that a preacher may use is somewhat limited. He is preaching on a subject rather than a theme. This means that he can conceivably run out of subjects after a time. This will limit the variety in his preaching. The topical method uses a short text or fragment of a text as the basis for the sermon, which can turn the hearer's focus away from the Bible and result in a more secular conclusion.

The freedom of the topical method is attractive to a fertile mind. It has a danger, however, which is inventiveness at the expense of scriptural authority.

Although topical preaching can be kept on a high level, it often descends to the level of the peripheral and sometimes even the sensational. It sometimes forsakes the timeless theme of the gospel to deal with timely topics that appeal to the popular imagination. This can be seen in the preaching of the late Harry Emerson Fosdick who has been referred to by many as the master of the topical method.

4. Methods in the traditional approach. Daniel P. Kidder in his book *A Treatise on Homiletics,* written in 1864, and Andrew Blackwood in his work entitled *The Preparation of Sermons,* written in 1848, give extensive coverage to topical preaching. There are several sermon plans that may be used in preparation for topical preaching.

a) The *selective* method is discussed by Frank Littorin in his book, *How to Preach the Word with Variety.* In this method several selected portions or verses from all parts of the Word are used. The preacher determines the theme and then searches through the entire Bible for its teaching. The subject or topical sermon may at times lack human interest because it grows out of sweeping surveys and often consists of vast abstractions. Even when topical preaching is at its best, founded upon Scripture and related to the needs and problems of the day, it still suffers from an inherent limitation. If the preacher selects his own theme upon the basis of his own preferences, he can hardly avoid being circumscribed by personal preferences. This hinders him in declaring to his congregation the "whole counsel of God."

b) The *adverbial* method was used effectively by Charles Spurgeon. He made use of a series of natural questions that he applied to the subject.

c) A. E. Garvie in his book *The Christian Preacher* discusses the *categorical* method. This makes use of categories of thought or patterns of thinking. One of the most common patterns is that of the time pattern involving past, present, and future. The categorical method of topical sermon organization is followed when the sermonizer uses one of the ten categories of thought listed earlier in this chapter (under "Subdivide Main Points," *Processes in subdivisions,*

5) as a guide for the discussion of the theme.

    d) The *deductive* method was a plan used by Phillips Brooks, Henry Ward Beecher, and others. They gave a brief discussion of the subject and then followed it with applications.

    5. Examples of the traditional approach. The following examples of topical outlines have been suggested by different homileticians.

Selective Method:
Title: "Readiness Is All"
  I. Eager to preach about Christ, Romans 1:15
  II. Eager to forgive in Christ, Ephesians 4:32
  III. Eager to die for Christ, 2 Timothy 4:6

Title: "Mountains of the Bible"
  I. The Mount of Revelation (Sinai), Exodus 20:1-17
  II. The Mount of Redemption (Calvary), Matthew 27
  III. The Mount of Discipleship (Horns of Hattin), Matthew 5-7
  IV. The Mount of Transfiguration (Hermon), Matthew 17:1-8

Adverbial Method:
Title: "Repentance"   Text: Acts 17:30
  I. What is repentance?
  II. Why is it necessary to repent?
  III. How can I benefit from repentance?

Categorical Method:
Title: "Christ Our Life"
  I. Its Source, John 1:4
  II. Its Giver, John 5:21; 10:28
  III. Its Sustainer, John 6:51
  IV. Its Object, Philippians 1:21

Deductive Method:
Title: "The Absurdity of Atheism"   Text: Psalm 14:1
  I. By its assertion that creation is without cause
  II. By its contradiction of the universal consciousness of man
  III. By its being the utterance only of the heart.

Additional Outlines:
Title: "Paul's Three Ambitions"
  I. To preach the gospel in untouched fields, Romans 15:20
  II. To be pleasing always to the Lord, 2 Corinthians 5:9
  III. To be faithful in the common duties of life, 1 Thessalonians 4:1

Title: "Peacemaking"   Text: Matthew 5:9
  I. The condition of peacemaking
  II. The character of peacemaking
  III. The cost of peacemaking

Title: "Watchman for the Morning"   Text: Psalm 130:6*b*
  I. The night watchman waits eagerly for the morning
  II. The night watchman waits confidently for the morning
  III. The night watchman waits patiently for the morning

The propositional approach. We have already noted several weaknesses in the traditional approach to topical preaching. Two of these outstanding weaknesses were its tendency toward breadth, which took away from its depth, and secondly, its tendency toward secularism. Incorporated within the revised approach are certain measures that diminish such weaknesses.

1. Features of the propositional approach.

a) Preach on a theme. In order to overcome the problem of excessive breadth, we should preach on a theme rather than on a subject. A subject is the broad topic such as "prayer." A theme is an aspect of a subject, such as "profits of prayer." A subject is normally one word, whereas a theme is a phrase.

b) Use a key word. The use of single key words for a message will also limit the breadth of the sermon. A key word is a plural noun that characterizes the main points of the message. If the subject of the message is "prayer" and the theme "the profits of prayer," then the key word might be *profits*. This would mean that each main point would be a profit gained from praying. A sample outline follows.

  I. Praying brings us into contact with God.
  II. Praying deepens our own spiritual life.
  III. Praying results in blessing for the ones for whom we pray
  IV. Praying prompts us to keep our lives free from known sin
  V. Praying brings us into closer fellowship with other believers

c) Employ scriptural undergirding. Another weakness we noted in the traditional approach was the tendency toward secularism rather than a scriptural foundation. In order to avoid this weakness the sermonizer should undergird the main truths of his message with Scripture. This Scripture should be selected in accordance with the truth presented and the context of Scripture in which it is located. The sermonizer will then ask, "Where in Scripture does it say directly or indirectly that prayer brings us into contact with God?" When this reference has been located, then it will be noted after the main point and quoted when the main point is presented to the listeners. If the point cannot be documented by Scripture it should not be preached.

2. Steps in the propositional approach. There are eight steps of sermon construction that might be employed in the construction of a topical outline.

Step 1. Subject: Soul-winning

Step 2. Theme: Reasons for being involved in soul-winning

Step 3. Proposition: Every Christian should be involved in soul-winning.

Step 4. Transitional Sentence: Every Christian should be involved in soul-winning because of the following reasons.

Step 5. Main Points:

    I. Because we can fulfill the command of Christ.

    II. Because we can have a part in presenting the message of life to a dying world.

    III. Because we can develop our own spiritual lives.

Step 6. Subpoints: Each of these will be logically related to the main point under which it is listed. The last subpoint in the series will be one of application that will show what the main point will mean in the daily life of the listeners.

Step 7. Introduction: The approach sentence might take the phrase "be involved" out of the proposition and begin the sermon by saying: "Many are willing to talk about and think about an activity, but are not willing to get involved in it." Note: There is no explanation as a part the introduction in the topical sermon outline because it is not based upon a single passage of Scripture.

Step 8. Conclusion: The objective sentence might read, "Therefore every Christian should be involved in soulwinning."

TEXTUAL PREACHING

The traditional approach.

1. Meaning of the traditional approach.The textual sermon is one that closely follows the language of the text. Its chief divisions are based on the principal words or clauses of that text. The text for such a sermon normally consists of just one verse. In some cases two successive verses may be used. This kind of sermon honors the Word of God by keeping near to it and dwelling upon it. It gradually develops the riches of the text.

The custom of founding religious discourse upon a text has prevailed ever since there has been a body of inspired Scripture from which to take a text. The word *text* comes from *texo* ("to weave") or from *textus* ("a web"). This indicates that the text is the web, tissue, or main thread of the discourse.

2. History of the traditional approach. Although the general historical use of texts or the founding of the sermon directly upon the Word of God may be traced back to the earliest ages, the modern use of the single, brief text as standing for the particular theme of the discourse is ascribed to the Presbyter Musaeus of Marseilles in the fifth century.

For the first twelve centuries of the Christian era the restriction of the text to an isolated Bible verse or a fragment of a verse was unknown. The topical sermon therefore was an innovation. Originally the Christian sermon was an exposition and only that. Restriction of the text to a verse or a fragment of a verse, which is common in the modern topical discourse, met with very strenuous opposition for two hundred years. It originated about 1200, and the older clergy of that date contested it stoutly.

The modern period of employing texts dates from the Reformation, at which time we find a return to ancient usage respecting the sources of texts. Another feature that characterized that period was a similar return to the ancient simplicity in the interpretation of texts. Some reject this simplicity of treatment, but it should be regarded as an asset rather than as a negative factor. It makes it easier for the preacher to memorize the outline and easier for the listeners to retain it.

Textual preaching is one of the most familiar and widely used methods. Two books that give a rather comprehensive coverage of the method are *Homiletics and Pastoral Theology*, by W. G. T. Sheed, written in 1867, and *Preaching Angles*, by Frank H. Caldwell, written in 1954.

3. Abuse of the traditional approach. Perhaps no method of sermonizing is subject to more serious abuse than the textual method. In some cases the method is made a refuge for ministerial idleness. The preacher degenerates into text-beating. Such a practice does not instruct or edify either the preacher or his congregation. Many other times narrowness and shallowness of treatment result from an excessive adherence to the textual method.

Since all the major divisions of the textual sermon must come from the one or two verses, Ilion T. Jones in *Principles and Practice of Preaching* suggests that it would be difficult to find one hundred texts in the whole Bible that would be adequate for the textual approach. J. A. Broadus reports that the Englishman John Howe preached fourteen sermons on the words, "We are saved by hope," taken from Romans 8:24, and delivered seventeen on 1 John 4:20 and eighteen on John 3:6. James Stewart would call this method of dealing with texts "textual vivisection."

4. Dangers of the traditional approach. There are numerous dangers inherent in textual preaching. One is the danger of *eisegesis*—the

temptation to read the message into a text rather than to draw the message out of the text. The text should not be used as a motto. In such a case the preacher selects a text just so the congregation will approve of the message because a text of Scripture has been attached to it. The sermon must be an outgrowth from the text rather than the text being fastened to the sermon. The sermonizer should avoid the temptation to prooftext. In such a case he uses the text to silence his opposition and compel assent rather than to unfold and apply a portion of the Word of God.

In developing the traditional textual sermon it is not considered necessary that the order of the words and phrases in the text establish the order for the divisions in the sermon. However, the text gives not only the theme of the sermon, but the essential steps of the development. It does not dictate the order of the steps. The textual method is closely allied to the expository. Like the expository message, the textual sermon should be contextual. It should have as its horizon nothing less than the whole biblical world, and its purpose nothing less than the mind of Christ. A text worthy of a week's work and the attention of a congregation should be central to biblical revelation. It should also be considered from the standpoint of the preacher's personal involvement with the text. The text, therefore, should be considered as to its place in God's Word and its relation to God's world.

5. Methods of the traditional approach. The following are some of the methods of developing the textual sermon in the traditional approach.

a) The *analytical* method is one of the most common methods used in formulating textual sermons. In this the text is separated into its various parts for the purpose of examination and consideration. The parts of the text discovered through analysis will then become the main points of the discourse.

> Title: "Waiting upon God"   Text: Isaiah 40:30-31
> I. They shall renew their strength
> II. They shall mount up with wings as eagles
> III. They shall run and not be weary
> IV. They shall walk and not faint

b) The *interrogative* method sees the content of the text in terms of questions it answers or questions that may be applied to it.

> Title: "A Blessed Discovery"   Text: Acts 11:23
> I. What did he see? "The grace of God"
> II. How did he feel? "He was glad"
> III. What did he say? "Cleave unto the Lord"

c) The *telescopic* method sees each succeeding point in the message as an extension of the preceding point. This means that the final point will be inclusive of all those that have preceded it.

> Title: "Certainty in Service"   Text: Romans 15:29
> I. I am coming to you with Christ
> II. I am coming to you with the gospel of Christt
> III. I am coming to you with the blessing of the gospel of Christ
> IV. I am coming to you with the fullness of the blessing of the gospel of Christ

d) The *implicational* method draws implications from words and phrases within the text and the implications provide the points of the message.

> Title: "The Great Provider"   Text: Psalm 145:16
> I. God provides personally: "Thou
> II. God provides easily: "Dost open Thy hand
> III. God provides abundantly: "And dost satisfy"

The propositional approach.
1. Unity in the propositional approach. One of the outstanding weaknesses of textual preaching according to the traditional approach is the tendency to have points without a unifying theme. Since unity is a necessary ingredient of a good sermon, the preacher should develop an approach to textual preaching that will provide for it.

The sermonizer must make certain that he has discovered the subject and the theme of the text. A careful study of the context will often give useful clues to the real theme of the individual text. It is imperative that the theme cover the entire verse rather than just one segment of it since each part of the verse must be related logically to the theme in order to have a unified message.

Another means of assuring unity in the message is to make certain that each of the parts of the text used as bases for the main points of the message be characterized by a single key word. Each sermon, whether it be topical, textual, or expository, should have a noun in the plural that homiletically is referred to as a *key word*. This key word characterizes the main points. This can be illustrated by turning to 2 Chronicles 7:14 and noting the three *benefits* (key word) for Christians when they turn to God.

> I. God will hear their prayer
> II. God will forgive their sin
> III. God will heal their land

When the main points of a textual sermon are not unified through the use of a key word, the tendency is to make each point a separate sermon by itself. If a message has three points, the preacher might be preaching three sermons instead of one.

2. Steps of the propositional approach. There are eight steps that might be followed in the development of a textual sermon.

Text: "Yet those who wait for the LORD will gain new strength, they will mount up with wings like eagles, they will run and not get tired, they will walk and not become weary" (Isa. 40:31).

Step 1. Subject: Waiting upon God

Step 2. Theme: The wisdom of waiting upon God

Step 3. Proposition: It is wise to wait upon God

Step 4. Transitional Sentence: Because of the blessings to be received, it is wise to wait upon God.

Step 5. Main Points:
   I. They who wait upon God have a change of strength (40:31*a*)
   II. They who wait upon God can live above the sordidness of life (40:31*b*)
   III. They who wait upon God have an extra endurance (40:31*c*)
   IV. They who wait upon God are adequate to face the daily routine of life (40:31*d*)

Step 6. Subpoints: Each of these will be logically related to the main point under which it is listed. The last subpoint in the series will be one of application, which will show what the main point will mean in the daily life of the listeners.

Step 7. Introduction: The approach sentence might take the word *wait* out of the proposition and begin the sermon by saying, "Waiting means many things to many different people." An explanation within the introduction will show the reason for using this particular theme for this verse.

Step 8. Conclusion: The objective sentence might read, "Therefore it is wise for every Christian to wait upon God."

NOTES

1. Warren Wiersbe and Lloyd Perry, *The Wycliffe Handbook of Preaching and Preachers* (Chicago: Moody Press, 1984), pp. 99-134.

2. Henry S. Coffin, *What to Preach* (New York: George H. Doran, 1926), p. 42.

3. Arthur Allen, *The Art of Preaching* (New York: Philosophical Library, 1943), p. 9.

4. A. W. Blackwood, *Expository Preaching for Today* (New York: Abingdon-Cokesbury, 1953), pp. 18-19.

5. G. Campbell Morgan, *The Westminster Pulpit*, 5 vols. (Westwood, N.J.: Fleming H. Revell, 1955), 1:7.

6. James R. Blackwood, *The Soul of Frederick W. Robertson* (New York: Harper, 1947), p. ix.

7. Joseph Parker, *These Sayings of Mine* (New York: Funk & Wagnalls, 1881), p. 7.

8. John Kelman, *The War and Preaching* (New Haven: Yale University, 1919), p. 151.

9. A. Skevington Wood, *The Art of Preaching* (Grand Rapids: Zondervan, 1963), pp. 54-55.

10. George W. Truett, *Sermons from Paul* (Nashville: Broadman, 1947), pp. 35-45.

BIBLIOGRAPHY

Bauman, J. Daniel. *Introduction to Contemporary Preaching.* Grand Rapids: Baker, 1972.

Braga, James. *How to Prepare Bible Messages.* Portland: Multnomah, 1969.

Brown, H. C., Jr., H. Gordon Clinard, and Jesse J. Northcutt. *Steps to the Sermon.* Nashville: Broadman, 1963.

Caemmerer, Richard R. *Preaching for the Church.* St. Louis: Concordia, 1959.

* Davis, H. G. *Design in Preaching.* Philadelphia: Muhlenberg, 1958.

Demaray, Donald E. *Proclaiming the Truth: Guides to Scriptural Preaching.* Grand Rapids: Baker, 1979.

Jones, Ilion T. *Principles and Practice of Preaching.* Nashville: Abingdon, 1956.

Koller, Charles W. *Expository Preaching Without Notes plus Sermons Preached Without Notes.* Grand Rapids: Baker, 1962.

Kroll, Woodrow Michael. *Prescription for Preaching.* Grand Rapids: Baker, 1980.

Mark, Harry C. *Patterns for Preaching: The Art of Making Sermons.* Grand Rapids: Zondervan, 1959.

O'Neal, Glenn. *Make the Bible Live.* Winona Lake, Ind.: BMH Books, 1972.

Perry, Lloyd M. *Biblical Sermon Guide.* Grand Rapids: Baker, 1970.

—————. *A Manual for Biblical Preaching.* Grand Rapids: Baker, 1965.

—————. *Biblical Preaching for Today's World.* Chicago: Moody, 1973.

Phelps, Austin. *The Theory of Preaching.* London: Dickenson, 1882.

Reu, J. M. *Homiletics: A Manual of the Theory and Practice of Preaching.* Grand Rapids: Baker, 1967.

* Robinson, Haddon W. *Biblical Preaching: The Development and Delivery of Expository Messages.* Grand Rapids: Baker, 1980.

Sangster, W. E. *The Craft of the Sermon.* Philadelphia: Westminster, 1936.

* Stott, John R. W. *Between Two Worlds: The Art of Preaching in the Twentieth Century.* Grand Rapids: Eerdmans, 1982.

* Vines, Jerry. *A Practical Guide to Sermon Preparation.* Chicago: Moody, 1985.

Whitesell, Faris D., and Lloyd M. Perry. *Variety in Your Preaching.* Westwood, N.J.: Revell, 1954.

4

BIBLICAL PREACHING AND SERMON VARIATION

The preacher is the man whose calling it is to create forms out of the most precious material which this earth provides. His material is the everlasting gospel, his tools are his full powers of thought and imagination, his object is to create a form which shall be the best possible to convey to other minds and imaginations the glory and beauty of that which he is seeking to portray. Possibly no conception of the preacher's task is greater than that which sets it forth as the work of the creative artist. (F. W. Dillistone, *The Significance of the Cross* [Philadelphia: Westminster, 1944], p. 180)

The secret of C. H. Spurgeon's power was that he believed in the Bible from cover to cover. Spurgeon preached from the whole Bible. Wisely, he varied the sermon plans from week to week so that no listener could complain that the sermons sounded alike. Like his Master, Spurgeon cultivated what he called the "surprise power."[1] A sermon without variety is as tiresome as driving on a highway that has no turns. Although the sermon may have the uniformity of excellence, it will bring a feeling of monotony to the listeners. The listener longs for diversity.

VARIETY IN SCRIPTURE MANAGEMENT

One method of gaining variety in preaching is by varying the manner of handling the Scripture. A homily is free and informal but not unstudied. This is usually a running commentary. It may be verse by verse or it may be a subject commentary. This type of message was used until the third century.

In the history of preaching, topical sermons have outnumbered all the other types. In such a message the theme is drawn from the text but is discussed independently of the text. It embraces a single leading idea that can be expressed in a terse proposition. Although topical preaching can be kept on a high level, it often does descend to the level of the peripheral and sometimes even to the sensational. The topical method of preaching originated about the year 1200. It is almost universally the method of the French pulpit. There are many varieties of topical plans. Spurgeon used the adverbial method. Phillips Brooks and Henry Ward Beecher gave a brief discussion and followed it with applications. This is referred to as the deductive method of topical preaching.

The textual manner of handling the text closely follows the language of the text, clause by clause, and word by word. Its chief divisions are based upon the principal words or clauses of the text. It is especially applicable to texts containing precepts, commands, promises, and warnings. Austin Phelps and Andrew Blackwood agree that normally the parts of a text are dealt with in the order of their presence in the text itself. Frank H. Caldwell suggests that the length of the passage being treated is the main distinction between the textual and the expository sermon.

The expository method of handling a passage of Scripture is sometimes referred to as explicatory preaching and sometimes as exegetical preaching. Such a sermon should present the results of exegesis and not the processes. This type of method aims at making a passage of Scripture plain to the hearer's mind and heart. It not only makes ancient truth clear but brings it into the present.

Writers of homiletical textbooks have used many different names for variations of these four basic methods for handling Scripture. Blackwood and Harry C. Mark refer to the adverbial or interrogative sermon. This sermon structure involves the division of the subject or text by applying interrogative words. Such words as who, what, why, where, and how are often used to obtain the main points of the message. Several of these may be used in a single sermon.

Illion T. Jones and Halford E. Luccock refer to the chase technique or guessing game sermon. This sermon explores a problem in pursuit of a solution. The sermon structure consists of a series of questions and answers related to a problem.

Mark refers to a two-point sermon called a couplet sermon. Each part is related to the other. The first consists of an exhortation, and the second is a related promise or practice.

Luccock and W. E. Sangster refer to a facet or jewel sermon. This sermon takes one idea and then shows by relationships and applications the relevance of this idea to experience. The faceting process may involve emphases of origin, consequences, implications, or concrete instances.

Blackwood, Jones, and Gerald R. Jordan refer to the Hegelian sermon (named after Georg Hegel). The structure has three main divisions. The first states the thesis, the second states the antithesis, and the third states the synthesis or truth that emerges from the conflict of points one and two.

Frank Littorin, Jones, Luccock, and Mark refer to the ladder, telescopic, oratorical, or pyramid sermon. This sermon structure is one in which each main division grows out of or builds upon the previous point. Each point carries the subject out a little farther similar to the unfolding of a telescope or the building of a ladder.

Other variations in sermonic structure could be added to this list, but these provide an insight into some of the varieties proposed by the various homileticians. A reading of some of the following books will provide the ways and means of constructing these and additional types.

Andrew W. Blackwood, *The Preparation of Sermons,* pp. 148-49.
Harry C. Mark, *Patterns for Preaching,* pp. 82-86, 98-102, 129-48.
Ilion Tingal Jones, *Principles and Practice of Preaching,* pp. 104-107.
Halford E. Luccock, *In the Minister's Workshop,* pp. 143-45, 134-37.
W. E. Sangster, *The Craft of the Sermon,* pp. 84-87.
Gerald Ray Jordan, *You Can Preach,* pp. 226-38.
Frank Littorin, *How to Preach the Word with Variety,* pp. 134-37.

Variety in Subject Matter

BIOGRAPHICAL PREACHING

History of biographical preaching. Biographical preaching has been popular in many periods of the history of preaching. The following six preachers are among the best known for such preaching.

Joseph Hall (1574-1656)
Alexander Whyte (1836-1921)
John Alexander Hutton (1868-1947)
F. W. Boreham (1879-1957)
Clarence Macartney (1879-1957)
Clovis Chappell (1882-1972)

Data in biographical preaching. The preacher will find it helpful to answer the following questions regarding the particular Bible character he plans to present in a sermon. The answers should be noted in written form so that they may be filed, as well as being available for use in the particular sermon at hand.

What sort of person was this?

What made him this sort of person?

What resulted from his being this sort of person?

What were the causes, preventatives, and cures of his weaknesses?

What were the secrets of his virtues?

How would you outline the character's life chronologically?

What is the meaning of the individual's name?

What is the ancestral background of the individual?

What significant religious and secular crises occurred in his life?

What advantages for personal development were enjoyed by this individual?

What traits of character were manifest?

What important friends did this character have?

What important influence did this individual exert?

What failures and faults occurred in this character's life?

What important contributions were made by this individual?

What one main lesson can be found within this life that is of special value to you?

What was the influence of the locality from the standpoint of geography, history, and culture upon this individual?

If this individual were in our present society, what would be his occupational or professional status?

What was this individual's relationship to God?

How can the gospel message be evidenced through this character?

How does this Bible character relate to the lives of the people who will be listening to this sermon?

With what enemies did he have to contend?

What motives were evidenced in the building of his life?

Values of biographical preaching. A wealth of material exists for the purpose of biographical preaching. Preaching on Bible characters gives the preacher an opportunity to set forth in a clear fashion the modern counterpart of the experience of a biblical person. The use of this type of subject matter helps make the Scriptures come alive with real persons who faced real situations and with whose lives, difficulties, hopes, and relationships God was immediately concerned and intimately involved.

Varieties of biographical preaching.

A *character sketch* sermon deals with the inner life of the Bible character. Each main point of the sermon is a characteristic.

A *life principle* sermon deals with the outstanding experiences of the character's life. The sermonizer determines the one activity or characteristic which was emphasized in the greatest number of the experiences. The key word for such a sermon might be "examples" or "evidences."

An *individual contribution* sermon deals with the abiding value of the career of a Bible character. The key word for such a sermon would be "contributions." Paul, for example, made contributions in the areas of missions, church life, and literature.

A *biblical conversation* sermon would highlight the parts of the conversation.

A *family life* sermon focuses on births, funerals, and marriages of Bible characters.

Several other starting points for preaching on Bible characters might include:

Conversations	Questions of Bible characters
Soul-winners of the Bible	Intercessors of the Bible
Confessions of Bible characters	Bible epitaphs
Fools of the Bible	Bible romances
Bible spies	Trials of Bible people

HISTORICAL /GEOGRAPHICAL PREACHING

Suggestions for historical/geographical preaching. Biblical history and geography provide a wide variety of material for sermons. The preacher's primary interest is not history but the God in history. To get a unifying subject from a historical passage, the sermonizer must take a far sweep of the mind both broad and deep. The task of the preacher is twofold in every sermon. First, he desires to give knowledge, and then he desires to produce faith. This type of sermon attempts to transform history and geography into precept.

The preacher may find help in trying to understand a historical passage of Scripture by answering the following questions.

Why was this passage included in Scripture in the first place?
What does God seem to be saying to the people of our day through the events in this passage?
How could we outline the chronological unfolding of this entire passage?
What are the time limitations of this segment of Bible history, and what other events were taking place at about this same period of time?
What do you know about the people who were involved in this segment of history?
What have you learned about the nature and actions of God as a result of studying this segment of Bible history?

How would you outline this portion of history?

Are there familiar verses within this segment which you've memorized or heard quoted through the years?

Is there a command, promise, or lesson which seems to summarize the practical preaching of the passage?

Are there words or phrases which are repeated several times throughout the passage?

Ideas for historical/geographical sermons. The following list suggests some of the types of historical/geographical material that can be used as bases for sermons.

1. Ideas for historical sermons.

a) A period of biblical history. Select a portion of Scripture that covers a rather extended period of biblical history. Select a principle or characteristic representative of the whole period.This can be accomplished by noting the outstanding high points of the period and finding a common denominator that ties these together. The truths emphasized in the message must not only have relevance for the historical period but must be shown to be relevant today.

b) An historical turning point. This sermon grows out of a decision made by an individual, a tribe of people, a nation, or a church.

c) A battle of the Bible. Determine the important causes leading up to the conflict. Were there any unique features involved in the actual battle? What were the results of the battle? What spiritual truths can be learned from this battle?

d) Several other starting points for preaching on historical material might include:

A biblical revival   A biblical church
A biblical apostasy   A biblical judgment

2. Ideas for geographical sermons.

a) A geographical location. The meaning of the actual name of the location may give a clue as to the importance of the location in Bible history. How would you characterize this location in terms of what transpired there? Why do we as Bible scholars remember this location?

b) A journey of the Bible. This is based upon the scriptural record of a journey taken by a prophet, tribe, or nation. Take special note of the high points in the journey. What basic truth for daily living do you find as you follow the progress of this trip?

c) A mountain of the Bible. Because of events that transpired at those locations, certain mountains in Scripture seem to possess inherent spiritual significance relating to the purposes of God.

DIDACTIC PREACHING

Difficulty of didactic sermons. Didactic sermons deal with biblical material that can be especially adapted for teaching as well as for preaching. In many of these types, the modern application is difficult to develop. It is often easier to teach the facts contained in the biblical account and then avoid the task of wrestling with the application by merely saying at the close, "You make your own application." Some of the material is difficult to put into sermonic form because it involves hermeneutics as well as homiletics if the preacher is to present the message in terms of its timeless meaning.

Variations of didactic sermons.

1. A parable sermon. This is based upon Scripture designed to impress a spiritual truth by the comparison or contrast of that truth with some object or incident. Preaching from parables helps to show the harmony that exists between the physical and the spiritual world. Such a sermon helps to make the truth more attractive and hence more easily remembered. It is wise to look at the immediate context for clues that may lead to the real meaning of the parable. Do not press every detail of the parable to the point of absurdity.

2. A beatitude sermon. This is based upon a verse or passage of either the Old Testament or the New Testament that begins with the word "Blessed." Note that when Christ gives a beatitude He states a condition and then a reward to the person if he attains this condition. Many beatitudes are found in the New Testament and many in the Old Testament, such as in Psalms 32, 41, and 119.

3. A typology sermon. This is one that appeals to the curiosity of many people. The use of this type of sermon helps to demonstrate the unity of the Bible by showing that Old Testament people and duties were foreshadows of the fullness of God's revelation in Christ. The preacher should be aware of the fact that this type of sermon involves hermeneutics as well as homiletics. Beware of making the sermon a journey into the mystery of typology without making a practical application for daily living.

4. A miracle sermon. This involves not only homiletics but also hermeneutics and in some cases special theological interpretation. Some preachers try to avoid this challenge by merely telling the miracle. In such cases they are merely teaching a lesson in history rather than preaching a sermon that would combine exposition with application.

There are several other types of didactic material that could be used for sermon starters.

A Bible prayer (John 17:1-26 or 2 Kings 19:14-19)
A Bible hymn (Ex. 15:1-21 or Rev. 5:6-10)

A Bible vision (Ezek. 37:1-14 or Rev. 1:9-20)
Names of deity (Gen. 22:14 or Judg. 6:24)
A Bible analogy (Rev. 22:16)
A Bible benediction (2 Thess. 3:16)
A night scene (Dan. 5:1-30)
A poetical portion (Ps. 1:1-6)

VARIETY IN PREACHING UNITS

BIBLE BOOK

There is a need for congregations to obtain a grasp of the main message of the various Bible books. This is especially true of new believers. When they have had a telescopic view of a whole Bible book, they will then be better able to understand at a later time the meaning of smaller passages within the larger context.

Text: Ruth   Title: Triumphant Faith
Text: Esther   Title: The Protection of
           Providence
Text: James   Title: Practical Christianity

BIBLE CHAPTER

Since there are 1,189 chapters in the Bible, the preacher has plenty of resource material for individual sermons or many series of sermons on chapters of the Bible.

Text: Psalm 19   Title: How God Speaks
Text: Hebrews 11 Title: Faith in Action
Text: Luke 15   Title: The Lost and Found
           Department

BIBLE PARAGRAPH

A good paragraph consists of one main thought. The paragraph divisions in our modern Bible translations were not in the original manuscripts. They have, however, been carefully designated in our present Bibles as aids to understanding.

Text: Joshua 1:1-9 Title: Secrets of Success
Text: Philippians 4:4-7 Title: A Prescription for
           Peace

BIBLE VERSE

Many of the 31,176 individual verses in the Bible provide sermonic foundations. Such a sermon is referred to as a textual sermon. Many of these sermonic texts have been memorized by the listeners.

Text: Luke 9:23   Title: The Demands of
                              Discipleship
Text: John 14:27   Title: The Believer's Inheritance

BIBLE KEY WORD

Key words of the Bible are those words that gain prominence often due to repetition but sometimes because of far-reaching meaning or significance. For these reasons such words often form the bases for sermons.

Straightway occurs forty-two times in the gospel of Mark.
Better occurs twelve times in the book of Hebrews.

VARIETY IN STARTING SOURCES

The starting idea for some sermons is located outside of Scripture. The idea is then related to the timeless truth of the Bible. The development of the sermon combines factors found in the extrabiblical source that can be related very clearly to the truth of the Word of God.

One might look at the extrabiblical item as a source of illustrative material for Bible truth.The extrabiblical source must be viewed as being only a vehicle to present the truth of Scripture.

CHRISTIAN CLASSICS
Pilgrim's Progress, by John Bunyan
The Practice of the Presence of God, by Brother Laurence
The Three-Fold Secret of the Holy Spirit, by James H. McConkey

GREAT HYMNS
"Beneath the Cross of Jesus": The Shadow of the Cross
"When I Survey the Wondrous Cross": The Wonder of the
    Cross
"I Need Thee Every Hour": The Blessing of His Presence

GREAT POEMS
"The Hound of Heaven," by Francis Thompson
"Live Christ," by John Oxenham
"And Christ Is Crucified Anew," by John Moreland

FAMOUS SLOGANS
"Stand firm!" by the Duke of Wellington at Waterloo
"I only regret that I have but one life to give for my country,"
    by Nathan Hale

OBJECTS OR HOBBIES
> Faces on coins (Luke 20:24)
> Coins and fish (Matt. 17:27)
> Hidden treasure (Matt. 25:18)

GREAT PAINTINGS
> *The Light of the World,* by Holman Hunt
> *The Last Supper,* by Leonardo DaVinci
> *Christ Before Pilate,* by Michael Munkacsy

The basis for each main point within such a sermon will be obtained from the extrabiblical source, but this will be shown to be in accord with the general teaching and emphasis of Scripture.

There are a number of suggestions and texts for the preacher at the end of this book (Appendix: Sermon Ideas for a Year in the Word).

Variety in the Preaching Program

INTRODUCTION TO A PREACHING PROGRAM

Need of a preaching program. Many preachers have experienced the frustration of coming to the point of working on the next scheduled message with no idea of where to begin. The responsibilities of the pastorate, the complexity of life, and unexpected events often keep us from the continuing preparation that will provide ideas for future messages. It is therefore profitable to set aside time for planning a preaching program.

A planned preaching program saves time and tends to give peace of mind. It guides the preacher in his study and tends to inspire a teaching ministry. There is an encouragement in such a program to work for variety. A partial preaching program of miscellaneous subjects is found at the end of this volume (Appendix: Sermon Ideas for a Year in the Word).

Planning a preaching program. As a starting point, the preacher should make a chart for each of the following twelve months, allocating spaces for each Sunday morning, Sunday evening, and midweek service. Some of the guidelines listed below will help him project possible subjects to be dealt with at those times when a message must be ready for presentation.

1. The Christian calendar. The first principle the preacher may use is that of the Christian year that embraces the chief events in the history of salvation. The book of Scripture readings for the Christian year is called a lectionary. The reading for any given

Sunday is called a pericope. The periocoptic system can be traced back to about A.D. 600. The pericope consists of a number of select verses expressing a unified thought focusing on certain festival days or seasons.

This plan commemorates seasons such as Advent, Epiphany, Lent, Easter, Ascension, and Pentecost.

Advent heightens our sense of waiting, expectation, and promise—and waiting is a large part of life. Daily, we await the birth of Jesus in our hearts, and we anticipate seeing Him in new ways in our lives. Advent, as a liturgical season, is a moment in the church's worship calendar which attunes us more sensitively to that part of our lives that is always advent—that is always waiting, expecting, and hoping.

Christmas celebrates all of those moments in our lives when waiting has been fulfilled in events. Christmas is the promise fulfilled; God does not leave us alone. We see God in Jesus, "with our own eyes," the Christmas preface says. Christmas is a good day to preach on the many ways in which God breaks into our world as He becomes one of us and reveals Himself in Jesus.

Epiphany lends itself to the same theme—the many showings of Jesus, and the recognition of Him as Messiah by wise men from another religious culture. We jump from the Christmas theme of Jesus being born into our lives to the ways in which we, in our lives, manifest Jesus to others. We move from Advent (expectation) to Christmas (birth) to Epiphany (manifestation).

Lent, Palm Sunday, Good Friday, and Easter are good times to preach on the place of sacrificial love and repentance in a lived dynamic religion. Its themes place conversion at the center of faith so that we may experience the many ways in which the risen Lord calls us daily from dyings and deaths to hopes for new directions, new ways of seeing things, and new faith energies.

Ascension Day and Pentecost invite sermons that focus on the ways in which we experience renewal and recreation in our lives.

2. The expositional plan. Some pastors select three or four books of the Bible they plan to cover rather extensively in their preaching program for the year. There is a danger that should be noted at this point. Many preachers stay in one book for too long a period of time. The listeners may lose interest. These types of messages may be repetitious in content and emphasis. If the preacher were using this principle and preaching from the book of Romans, he might use the first eight chapters during one section of his preaching program the first year. He could then use chapters nine through eleven as a segment of his preaching program in the second year and chapters twelve through sixteen during the third year.

3. The denominational arrangement. Sometimes special emphases have been assigned to each of the twelve months by denominational planners. The following model is a sample of the kind of preaching program a denominational fellowship might suggest to its ministers.

MONTH	SPECIAL DATES	SPECIAL THEMES

JANUARY
Special Emphasis:
  Bible Study
	1 Day of Prayer
	6 Day of Epiphany
	
	25 Forefather's Day
		Missionary Sunday
		Christian Education
		  Week
		National Youth Week
		First Week: Week of
		  Prayer

FEBRUARY
Special Emphasis:
  Christian Education
	14 Sweetheart's Day	First Sunday: Boy
		  Scouts; Youth
		Second Sunday: Brotherhood
		  and Race Relations;
		  Christian World
		  Fellowship
		Third Sunday: Christian
		  Education

MARCH
Special Emphasis:
  Home Missions
		First Sunday: National
		  Missions

APRIL
Special Emphases:
  Life Commitment;
  Christian Vocation
	19 Patriot's Day	First Sunday: Renewal
		  Life Commitment;
		  Christian Stewardship

MAY
Special Emphasis:
  Christian Home
	30 Memorial Day	First Week: Christian
		  Family
		Second Sunday: Mother's
		  Day
		National Music Week

JUNE
Special Emphases:
  Youth; Vacation
  Bible School
		First Sunday: Christian
		  Unity
		Second Sunday: Children's
		  Day
		Third Sunday: Father's Day
		Last Sunday: Nature; Flag
		  Day; Trinity Sunday

Continued:

MONTH	SPECIAL DATES	SPECIAL THEMES

JULY
Special Emphases:
  Church Camps;
  Christian
    Recreation;
  Christian
    Literature
	4 Independence Day	Second Sunday:
		  Christian Literature;
		  Freedom Sunday

AUGUST
Special Emphases:
  Leadership
    Enlistment;
  Church Library;
  Church Renewal
	4 Transfiguration Day
	15 Friendship Day	

SEPTEMBER
Special Emphasis:
  Church Program
  Planning
		First Monday: Labor Day
		Second Sunday: Public
		  Education and College
		Third Sunday: Church
		  Sunday Rally Day
		Last Sunday: Leadership
		  Commitment Sunday
		National Home Week
		National Fall Sunday
		  School Week

OCTOBER
Special Emphasis:
  Teaching and
  Training in Church
  Membership
	12 Columbus Day
	31 Reformation Day
		First full week: Christian
		  Education Week
		First Sunday: Worldwide
		  Communion Sunday
		Third Sunday: Layman's
		  Sunday;
		National Bible Week
		Girl Scout Week

NOVEMBER
Special Emphases:
  Christian
    Stewardship;
  Men and Missions;
  International
    Good Will
	1 All Saints' Day
	11 Armistice Day
	  (Veterans' Day)
		Stewardship Sunday
		Election Day
		Second Sunday: World
		  Peace Sunday
		Fourth Thursday:
		  Thanksgiving Day
		American Education Week
		National Book Week

Continued:

MONTH	SPECIAL DATES	SPECIAL THEMES

DECEMBER
Special Emphases:
  World (Foreign)
  Missions;
  Worldwide Bible
  Reading
	15 Bill of Rights Day
	25 Christmas Day	

ADVANTAGES OF A PREACHING PROGRAM

The program offsets the unexpected. Interruptions such as funerals, weddings, visitors, telephone calls, salesmen, and conferences all combine to upset the pastor's plans for thorough study and unhurried sermon preparation. These disturbances are less distracting when the preacher already has his sermons well under way because of careful planning.

The program encourages thorough study. As a teacher prepares and follows a course of study, even so a preacher must plan to teach the fundamental doctrines of the Christian faith, the contributions of the Bible personages, and the messages of the books of the Bible; in short, he must be able to teach the "whole counsel of God." This requires a teaching ministry and a planned program.

The program can focus on emphases demanded by the church schedule. The preacher who looks ahead and plans his preaching to fit the seasons of the year, special days, and the special emphases of the church calendar will have his preaching better adjusted than the man who does not.

The program makes for variety. The basic purpose of planning a preaching program is to include a wide variety of subjects, emphases, and types of sermons. This variety can also be seen in encouraging the preacher to make use of many books of the Bible in the course of a year's preaching.

The program provides a permanent record. For future reference, the preacher has the date, title, and Scripture reading for every sermon preached.

The program aids the music of the church. A planned preaching program encourages preparation for special vocal and instrumental music as well as careful selection of hymns that closely relate to the message.

The program prevents undue overlapping of subject matter. The program encourages a correlation between the teaching of the pulpit and the church school.

The program is a timesaving device. The time the preacher normally would spend hunting for sermon ideas may now be given to direct preparation on his predetermined theme.

The program prevents frustration. The preacher sleeps better and works better when he has his sermons planned weeks ahead.

INFLUENCES ON A PREACHING PROGRAM

God's guidance. As in the process of sermon construction so the planning of the preaching program begins when the preacher's heart, head, and hands are in contact with God. The preacher recognizes the guidance of the Holy Spirit as he seeks to adequately plan his program.

Civic holidays. In his preaching program the preacher must make provision for both local and national holidays. Whether it be Evacuation Day for the Bostonian preacher or an October Thanksgiving for the Canadian preacher, these, together with Memorial Day, Independence Day, and many other holidays must carefully be considered.

Church occasions. Every local church upon occasion celebrates its anniversary, dedicates some piece of its property, or remembers Children's Day. Such occasions must find proper place in the minister's preaching program.

Vacation periods. In addition to one month's vacation in the summer, some preachers take one right after Christmas or Easter. When planning his preaching program, every pastor must decide what weeks he is planning for vacation.

Education conferences. Many up-to-date churches have annual Christian education conferences. Each pastor must decide if this factor will influence his preaching program.

Missionary conference. Most pastors incorporate some form of missionary conference into their church at least once a year. The dates and speakers must be carefully noted within the preaching program.

Guest speakers. When the preacher is on vacation or when a noted speaker is to fill the pulpit as a guest speaker, provision must be made in advance.

Subgroup variety. No preaching program should be planned apart from having sermonic material adaptable to men, women, and children. The preacher must plan to have something in his sermon for everyone present.

Church program. The pastor must plan his preaching program in light of the total local church program. Provisions must be made for baptism, communion, and choir concerts. The program of the church school, and men's, women's, and youth organizations all must be considered in order that the program will be integrated and free from overlapping.

Preacher's personality. Some preachers may be gifted in the area of dialogue or dramatics; others may have talents in the field of music or art. This factor will have an important part to play in the variety and type of sermons used within the preaching program.

Community emphases. When planning his preaching program, the preacher must be aware of significant community emphases during the course of the year. A special drive such as Heart Sunday, a new development of homes, an athletic venture, an educational or professional conference—all will be factors for the preacher to consider.

Evangelistic campaign. If the preacher is to include an evangelistic campaign during the course of the year, the date, time, and speaker will all be factors to consider when planning the preaching program.

Bible conferences. During the summer months a pastor may be asked to preach at a Bible conference. Whether the messages are to be evangelistic, devotional, or instructional in nature is just one of the many questions a preaching program will determine.

Prophecy conferences. In recent years prophecy conferences have become very popular in the local church. A planned preaching program will not only consider the particular Bible prophecy to be discussed but also the dates and speakers for the conference.

PRINCIPLES FOR A PREACHING PROGRAM

Christian calendar principle. Even though the principle of the Christian calendar is used chiefly by Roman Catholics, Anglicans, Episcopalians, Lutherans, and other liturgical groups, there are great values and possibilities in it for nonliturgical churches. At least in a modified way this principle can extend the effectiveness of evangelical preaching. A description of this plan has been given earlier in this chapter.

Bible survey principle. The preacher gives his people an overall picture of some section of the Bible each month or uses some other type of chronological sequence. This is an excellent principle for the preacher to employ when desirous of having the congregation carry their Bibles to church with them.

"Trends of the times" principle. Through a close following of periodicals and books, the pastor, while preaching on current developments in religion, morals, politics, economics, education, athletics, or world affairs, relates these to biblical truth. This principle provides the preacher with a good opportunity to preach from Bible prophecy.

Denominational principle. Most of the major denominations publish and send to their pastors various guides and suggestions for planning a preaching program. (See the model under the earlier section "The denominational arrangement" within the subdivision *Introduction to the Preaching Program.*)

Sermonic principle. Whether in the morning service or evening service, the pastor keeps preaching a series of sermons. Various types of Bible material such as characters, doctrines, or miracles may be the basis for the series.

Unit principle. This principle is similar to that of the teacher who plans his lessons in units. For the preacher, an emphasis upon a certain subject is maintained for a period of time (unit). For example, the preacher may present a unit lasting one month on "Stewardship of Money" and "Stewardship of Talents."

Sermon-type principle. Various sermon types such as character sketches, interesting incidents, journeys of the Bible, night scenes, prayers, or great hymns may be employed by the preacher. A thorough presentation of these and many other sermon types are found in *Variety in Biblical Preaching*, by Lloyd M. Perry and Bruce L. Strickland (Peabody, Mass.: Powell, 1959).

Eclectic principle. During each year the preacher may wish to use a variety of principles for his preaching program. This may be done by combining several of the principles set forth above

LAYOUT OF A PREACHING PROGRAM

Mechanics of the layout. During the preacher's summer vacation is probably the best time for the layout of his preaching program. This may be set up in one of two ways: the preacher may formulate a chart capable of being mimeographed on which the preaching program will be recorded, or he may purchase a workbook for this purpose, such as the *Pastor's Complete Workbook*, compiled by Charles Merrill Smith (New York: Abingdon).

Elements of the layout. The following items should be included in the layout of any preaching program.

Notation of all services including Sunday (both morning and evening), prayer meeting, and special days
The title and/or theme of the sermon
The main points of the sermon
The Scripture passage to be read
The responsive reading (if any)
Hymns and special music

VARIETY IN THE COMMUNICATION PROCESS

New view of sermonic communication. The conventional sermon conceives of communication as a one-way process. This originates in a transmission theory of education wherein truth transfer is automatic. Both the preacher and his people suffer when such a process is exclusively employed. The preacher feels threatened by advances being made in the field of secular mass communication media. He feels frustrated since he feels that he is not getting through to his people in a way that encourages a change in their living.

Communication is not a one-way process, but is rather a complex, two-way relationship. The word "communication" is derived from the Latin *communis,* meaning "common." To communicate is to establish a "commonness" with the receiver. It involves the sharing of information, ideas, and attitudes.

Biblical examples of sermonic communication. A study of the methods of communication of the Word of God in biblical times reveals that the method differed from the typical lecture-sermon of our present day. Preaching consisted of reading a passage of Scripture followed by clarification or exposition. In the service any qualified person was permitted to speak, argue, or discuss.

1. The example of Christ. Jesus preached few sermons like the conventional sermons preached today. Of some 125 incidents recorded in the gospels wherein Jesus communicated with people, about fifty-four were initiated by the auditors. His communication was characterized by a conversation with questions and answers, objections, debate, agreement, and rejection.

2. The example of the apostles. The apostles also engaged in multilateral preaching. They disputed in the synagogues (Acts 17:17; 18:4) and "in reasoning daily" in the school of Tyrannus (Acts 19:9). From a study of the sermons of these men we gather that the auditors were free to interact with them. William B. Thompson, in *Listener's Guide to Preaching,* writes: "The first Christians, as you know were Jews. After their conversion to Christianity, they had no reason to change their basic pattern of worship—only their interpretation of the scriptures. Even the Gentile converts took over the rather informal synagogue worship in which the people sang songs, prayed, read scriptures and shared in interpreting them."[2]

He then goes on to say, "It did not occur to the very first Christians to delegate the responsibility for preaching or officiating in worship exclusively to one of their members. The entire church shared the responsibility."[3] Not only does the Bible commend multilateral preaching, but our day seems to demand it.

Suggested changes of sermonic communication. The change from the monological presentation to that of a cooperative approach involves a change of method but does not demand a change in the basic message. Irrespective of the method used, the message must have the contents of the Christian faith.

Cooperative preaching or dialogical preaching will encourage the laymen in our churches to share their convictions and experiences with others. This type of presentation can be one in which feelings and concerns are shared and trust can emerge.

Preparing for cooperative preaching demands more time and work than preparing for conventional preaching. It takes more time to prepare the different methodology of delivery, It also takes more time to discover and arrange the content.

Various stimuli in sermonic communication. Discussion is stimulated when the preacher surveys the past in search of timeless truths. History does not repeat itself exactly. Today is always different from yesterday. There are, however, certain timeless principles running as threads through the cloth of time. Since God is changeless, it is profitable for the sermonizer to seek to discover what the scriptural account teaches about the changeless God. What is God like? How does God work? What is God doing? What is God trying to teach us? Profitable discussions can arise as the sermonizer, together with his congregation, seeks to discover the teachings of the passage about God.

Discussion is stimulated as the sermonizer and his congregation seek to establish the original purpose behind the presentation of the passage of Scripture when it was first conveyed and the relevance of that purpose to our present day. In some cases the purpose is clearly stated in Scripture.

Discussion is stimulated as the sermonizer and his congregation seek methods of applying timeless principles to present day living. Many conventional sermons are weak in the area of application. People in different occupations apply principles in different ways. To the doctor it means one thing, but to the school teacher it may mean something else. The sermonizer must strive to see life through the eyes of his listeners and be prepared to show possible methods for the application of truth to life.

Discussion is stimulated as the sermonizer and his congregation survey the implications of scriptural segments and their timeless truths. The denotation or literal meaning of a word, for instance, can be discovered in the dictionary or lexicon. We look it up, read it, and there the matter closes. The connotation of a word involves the suggestive emotional content and significance of a word beyond its literal meaning. This type of meaning gives us something to discuss.

Discussion is stimulated as the sermonizer preaches sermons that help the congregation discover biblical answers for present day problems. These should be problems related to the living of the immediate congregation. Some have suggested that each sermon should be designed to solve some problem. Others have suggested that each sermon should be designed to answer a question. If such a procedure is followed, the sermonizer would make certain that the question the sermon seeks to answer is a question someone in the congregation is asking. Maybe we spend too much time trying to answer questions no one is asking.

NOTES

1. Charles H. Spurgeon, *Great Pulpit Masters* (New York: Revell, 1949), 2:10-11.
2. William B. Thompson, *A Listener's Guide to Preaching* (Nashville: Abingdon, 1965), p. 32.
3. Ibid.

BIBLIOGRAPHY

Blackwood, Andrew Watterson. *Biographical Preaching for Today.* Nashville: Abingdon, 1954.

*_____ *Planning a Year's Pulpit Work.* New York: Abingdon, 1942.

* Brown, H. C., Jr. *A Quest for Reformation in Preaching.* Waco, Tex.: Word, 1968.

Caldwell, Frank H. *Preaching Angles.* Nashville: Abingdon, 1954.

Davis, H. Grady. *Design for Preaching.* Philadelphia: Fortress, 1958.

Dunkle, William F., Jr. *Values in the Church Year.* New York: Abingdon, 1959.

Eggold, Henry J. *Preaching Is Dialogue.* Grand Rapids: Baker, 1980.

Forell, George W. *The Christian Year.* New York: Thomas Nelson, 1964.

Gibson, George Miles. *Planned Preaching.* Philadelphia: Westminster, 1954.

_____.*The Story of the Christian Year.* New York: Abingdon, 1964.

Hardin, H. G., et. al. *The Celebration of the Gospel.* New York: Abingdon, 1964.

Holcraft, Paul E. *Texts and Themes for the Christian Year.* New York: Abingdon, 1957.

Johnson, Howard A. *Preaching the Christian Year.* New York: Charles Scribner's, 1957.

Luccock, Halford E. *In the Minister's Workshop.* New York: Abingdon-Cokesbury, 1944.

MacLennan, David A. *Resources for Sermon Preparation.* Philadelphia: Westminster, 1957.

_____.*Preaching Week by Week.* Westwood, N. J.: Revell, 1963.

Massey, James Earl. *Designing the Sermon: Order and Movement in Preaching.* Nashville: Abingdon; Abingdon Preacher's Library, 1980.

Pearce, J. Winston. *Planning Your Preaching.* Nashville: Broadman, 1967.

Perry, Lloyd M. and Faris D. Whitesell. *Variety in Your Preaching.* Grand Rapids: Baker, 1965.

* Skinner, Craig. *The Teaching Ministry of the Pulpit.* Grand Rapids: Baker, 1973.

Steel, David. *Preaching Through the Year.* Atlanta: John Knox, 1973.

Stevenson, Dwight T. *In the Biblical Preacher's Workshop.* Nashville: Abingdon, 1967.

Tompson, William D., and Gordon C. Bennett. *Dialogue Preaching.* Valley Forge: Judson, 1969.

Wallis, Charles L. *Lenten-Easter Sourcebook.* New York: Abingdon, 1961.

5

BIBLICAL PREACHING AND CONTENT CLARIFICATION

Without order, incoherence makes it unintelligible. The educated person may indeed be able to disentangle your meaning from your chaotic expression, but the uneducated person will be bewildered, whereas if you observe just and well-considered order, the educated will appreciate it, and the uneducated will be able to understand. (Bishop Boyd Carpenter, *Lectures on Preaching,* quoted in Harold Ford, *The Art of Preaching* [London: Herbert Jenkins, 1926], pp. 56-57)

CLARIFICATION IN SERMONIC STYLE

MEANING OF STYLE

Etymology. The word *style* comes from the Latin *stylus,* which referred to the pointed iron pen with which the Romans wrote on their tablets. Style is one's manner of expressing thought, whether in writing or in speaking. It is the expression in language of the thought qualities and spirit of the man. It is his characteristic way of expressing his thoughts. It involves the use of the right words in the right places. Style is the manner as distinguished from the matter.

Method. Style is a medium through which the speaker tries to secure a response. It represents the way in which a language pattern is used under a given set of conditions. It becomes the instrument through which ideas become meaningful. The expression the speaker gives to his ideas, together with whatever rhetorical devices he uses to enhance his effectiveness, may be called his style.

Style was one component of the classical rhetoric, the others being invention, arrangement, memory, and delivery. Style, therefore, referred to the process of phrasing in language the ideas that were invented and arranged.

Priority. The first and most urgent challenge of the public speaker is to make himself understood. In achieving this aim of communication through public address, no part of rhetoric is more difficult to master than style.

Charles E. Jefferson stated, "Next to the baptism of the Holy Spirit the most indispensable gift for every American preacher is a mastery of the English tongue. No time should be begrudged that is spent in perfecting the preacher's style."[1]

Style, or language, is important to the extent that it helps to prepare and subsequently to open the minds of the hearers. To be appropriate, language must be adapted to the personality of the speaker, to the type of message, to the audience, and to the occasion.

Subordination. The Sophists, who were the early speech teachers on the island of Sicily from 500 B.C. to approximately A.D. 100, stressed style as an end in itself. Their doctrine of plausibility made the winning of a case in the courts of more consequence than style as a factor in the speech itself. The stylists Longinus, Dionysius, and Demetrius, on the other hand, were not sophistic in their view of style. They regarded it as a part of the whole process of rhetoric and not as an end in itself.

Since the best style attracts the least attention to itself, only the most critical observer is likely to appreciate its excellence. The prevalent tendency is to attach greater significance to the matter presented than to the manner of presentation.

TYPES OF STYLE

Three classical works on style were written about A.D. 100. Dionysius wrote a twenty-six-chapter work entitled *On Literary Composition*. This was concerned with the style of public address. The work of Longinus had forty-four chapters and was more concerned with style as it pertained to poetry. A work by Demetrius was entitled *On Style*.

Three styles. A three-way classification of the types of style got its start as early as 85 B.C. with the publication of *Rhetorica Ad Herennium*, the earliest Roman work we know that is anywhere near its complete form. The three types were the grand, the middle, and the plain.

These were referred to by Cicero as being the three complexions of eloquence. When Quintilian adopted these three types, he defined the plain as being that adapted to the duty of stating facts, the grand as that given to the moving of feelings, and the middle as that of pleasing or conciliating. Gorgias (485-380 B.C.) developed the grand style and gave emphasis to figures of speech. Lysias (450-380 B.C.) emphasized the plain style and stressed the fact that the best art is that which conceals itself.

Four styles. Demetrius dealt with four main types of style. These four types were: the elevated, which made use of metaphors and comparisons; the elegant, which was noted for its charm and vivacity; the plain, noted for its clearness and simplicity; and the forcible style. Style to Demetrius included both dictation and composition.

TESTS FOR STYLE

Need for tests. There are certain influences which will tend to shape a preacher's style. One of these influences is culture. This will inevitably condition the character of his speech.

Another influence upon style, which is stressed by John Genung, is that of the subject matter. The technical content of the material will, for instance, have definite bearing upon the speaker's style of presentation. Personal character is revealed by the speaker's style of expression. A man speaks as he does because of what he is. "Out of the abundance of the heart the mouth speaketh."

Appropriateness is the most functional aspect of the whole problem of style. The mode of expression should be consistent with the nature of the message.

List of tests. Richard R. Caemmerer has suggested a list of tests for style which crystallize some of the mechanics of style in a succinct fashion. Some of these tests might be worded as follows:

> Are the subjects clear?
> Are the subjects and predicates close together?
> Are the pendent and rambling constructions few in number?
> Are there far more active than passive constructions?
> Are the subjects concrete and personal?
> Are the paragraphs unified?
> Are the summaries adequate so that the hearer will consciously move on to the next idea?
> Are the hearers left with a clear reminder of the goal and a clear application of the gospel as power?
> Are new ideas introduced slowly enough for the hearer to catch them?
> Are the definitions clear in terms of the preacher or in terms of the hearer?
> How many people in the audience will find it easy to listen to the message?
> Do the ideas march on promptly without too much backtracking?

Does the conclusion summon to resolution as well as to
  thought?
Does each paragraph have data that are sufficiently visual and
  applied?
Does the topic of each paragraph stand out clearly near the
  beginning?
Do the verbs suggest movement?

Greatest of tests. The greatest test of style, however, would
seem to be whether or not the style of the particular message con-
tributes fully to the communication of ideas and to the gaining of
the intended response. If you accept the principle that speech is for
communication, not exhibition, you will understand the value of
using language which is understandable to your listeners.

The great preachers of every age have not been like lawyers
arguing a case, or salesmen pushing a product; rather they have
been like poets seeking to suffuse the mind with light, to empower
the emotions with the splendor of revelation, and so to capture the
will of God.

It is helpful to listen to a good speaker for the purpose of
improving one's style. Such speakers may be heard on television or
radio. The program might be tape-recorded if desired, thus making
it available for study for some time to come.

The speaker should keep in mind the fact that his purpose is
to communicate ideas and not to display artifices. Style, or language, is important only to the extent that it helps to prepare the
minds of the listeners for the understanding and reception of his
ideas. The expression which he gives to this thought, together with
the rhetorical devices which he may use to strengthen his effectiveness, may be called his style.

QUALITIES OF STYLE

There are certain qualities of style which should be *avoided*
by the preacher. Ebenezer Porter lists these as being six in number.
He includes what he terms the theological dialect, the colloquial
dialect, the essay style, the formal style, a dull style, and sensationalism of style. It was Longinus who years before stated that the glar-
ing improprieties of language can be traced to a common root,
namely the pursuit of novelty in thought.

On the other hand at least six qualities of style should be *cultivated*: simplicity, strength, perspicuity, energy, beauty, and imagination.

Simplicity. The preacher will find that short sentences are
always easier to understand than long ones and that short words
are as important as short sentences. Deliberate variety in sentence
structure will serve to break any possible tendency to monotony.

The varied sentence structure will create mood without a noticeable attempt to force itself into the attention field of the listener. The tempo of the style will be affected by the sentence types as well as by sentence length.

Strive for economy of expression. Let one word do the work of two, a phrase the work of a clause, and a sentence the work of two or more sentences. Wordiness may decrease clarity by making the thought vague, by injecting irrelevant ideas, and by prolonging the development of a point.

Strength. Mastery of style is more a matter of absorption and ability to adjust to the needs of the audience than it is a matter of learning rules.

1. In sentences. The main thing to be desired in a sentence is strength. The subject should be kept close to the predicate. The mastery of the use of the periodic sentence is said to afford conclusive proof of a man's education and culture. The mixture of short and long sentences will add to force, clarity, and swiftness in the preparation of the material.

2. In words. There are certain general rules for style pertaining to words. One's words should be short and simple. It is well to be sparing in one's use of adjectives. The speaker should avoid *pleonasm*, or the use of more words than necessary to express the idea. The preacher will be wise to avoid slang words, vulgar words, colloquial words, hackneyed words, foreign words, barbarism, solecism, and exaggerated expressions. There are other types of words that should be used only sparingly. The list would include technical or scientific words, heavy theological words, philosophical words, abstract and ambiguous words. The speaker should concentrate on using simple words, plain words, picturesque words, concrete words, short words, vivid words, exact words, energetic words, euphonious words, pungent words, and words of action.

How can we improve our vocabularies? Techniques and formulas abound in this field. Some say, "Learn a new word each day," but few will carry through with this suggestion. Others suggest that you look up each new word when you encounter it, but this suggestion often proves impractical. Others suggest, "Look it up; write it down; use it seven times within the day."

It may be difficult, however, to maneuver the conversation so that you can use new words seven times within the day.

The principal methods for improving vocabulary are to read good literature, listen to cultured people, and speak and write. The adage, "We learn to do by doing" has special application to improving language style.

Robert J. McCracken has wisely said, "It is a misfortune when a preacher has no feeling for the magic of words and no flair for word-weaving. We should care for words, should select them judiciously and lovingly."[2] This zest for words can be enhanced through a study of the etymology and meaning of words. The wise use of the dictionary and thesaurus is essential. The small handbooks available for vocabulary building are valuable tools. A study of good poetry will sharpen one's taste for words that are expressive both through their meaning and their sound.

It is wise to give preference to sensuous words (words related to the five senses), rather than abstract words. It is wise to remember that strong nouns and verbs carry the weight of the thought. Adjectives and adverbs do not convey thought but merely color it. These should therefore be used sparingly.

3. In paragraphs. Good style demands that each paragraph begin with a key sentence that is clear and crisp. The remaining portion of the paragraph has as its purpose the explanation and enforcement of the idea contained in the opening sentence. Each paragraph contains one main idea with its development.

Perspicuity. George Campbell in his *Philosophy of Rhetoric* stated that the qualities of style that are strictly rhetorical are perspicuity, vivacity, elegance, animation, and music. Richard Whately stressed three qualities of style, namely perspicuity, energy, and elegance or beauty. The quality of energy is that which Campbell referred to as vivacity. Ebenezer Porter emphasized grammatical purity, perspicuity, strength, beauty, and sublimity. The classical tradition generally accepted four qualities of style, namely, correctness, clearness, ornateness, and propriety. Perspicuity, or clearness, would appear to be the first excellence of style.

It is wise to avoid the extremes of either conciseness or prolixity by making a careful use of repetition and illustration. Illustrations have as one of their basic purposes that of making one's meaning more clear. They also help people remember the truths taught, promote varied and continued application, awaken and sustain interest, and exert a force of proof that helps to persuade.

Perspicuity, which Hugh Blair defines as the conveying of ideas clearly, is hampered by the obscure and the unintelligible. These include the use of technical terms, long sentences, poor arrangement of material, and the use of the same word with different meanings. Theodore Ferris states that the preacher who cannot speak in terms that at least a high school student can understand should not speak at all.

The lectures on style written by Blair, emphasized three requirements for perspicuity. The first of these was purity of words and construction. The second was propriety. This involved the

selection of words according to the best usage. The third require-
ment was precision. The words used should express the idea and
no more.

Perspicuity, or clarity, begins in the mind of the preacher. It
involves his identity with the people as well as the structure of language. A logically arranged basic structure for the message will tend
to promote clarity. It is wise to reduce one's message to one concise, simple, timeless truth, known homiletically as the proposition.

Conversational style will aid clarity. The conversational style
of delivery was advanced in the public speaking field by James
Winans and in the field of pulpit address by Phillips Brooks. In this
style the speaker converses with his audience as a gentlemen converses with his friends.

This conversational style makes use of personal pronouns,
personal names, words of definite masculine and feminine gender,
and words of definite personal description. The language of direct,
oral discourse is marked by *I* and *you*, *we*, *our*, and *us*. It is marked
also by the more copious use of the question that most readers
would tolerate. Indeed, the use of interrogation and the first and
second person pronouns show unmistakably that audience and
speaker are face to face. It also uses what are known as personal
sentences, such as questions, commands, exclamations, direct and
indirect quotations, and sentences addressed directly to the audience. Contractions are also used in preference to the longer forms
of a written style.

Clearness includes the choice of words and their arrangement.
Quintilian regarded this as the first virtue of a composition.

Energy. Energy of style is promoted by conciseness. Energy, or
vivacity, depends upon the word choice, the number of words used,
and the arrangement of words. In choosing words, avoid abstract
and general terms. Make use of figures of speech. Metaphors are
preferred to plain comparisons. What made the old prophets such
powerful communicators of their vision? They reported it in concrete imagery, in metaphors and analogies that were close to the
soil and to the actualities of human existence. In arranging words,
it is wise to make use of periodic sentences.

The rhetorical question makes oral language more direct and
personal than written language. It motivates an audience to think
about the question. The use of short sentences, interrogative sentences, balanced sentences, and parallel structure will also help to
provide energy to style. Speakers and listeners alike know that the
commanding sentence, the lively word, the apt phrase, the vivid
metaphor, the amusing epithet, of all the elements of speech, often
make the most immediate and most enduring impression on listeners.

Beauty. In gaining beauty, or elegance of style, one must avoid smothering his work with ornamentation. The development of that terseness of expression known as the epigram, and the occasional use of antithesis will lend elegance. Of the six Yale lecturers who referred to elegance of style, only John Broadus spoke of it as being a desired characteristic.

Imagination. Consideration should be given to the cultivation of an imaginative style. Imagination is awakened and invigorated by communion with nature and contact with art and literature. The study of poetry develops penetrating vision, lofty aspiration, quick sympathies, concreteness of thought, and choice diction.

Cultivating the imagination in preaching is more than collecting illustrations and anecdotes. It is rather a habit of mind and a way of attending to the actualities of life.

DIFFERENCES IN STYLE

A preacher is a public speaker and not a public reader. As such his style should be the spoken rather than the written style. Skinner stated, "The style fitting for a public discourse is so different from that which becomes matter intended for the press that, if it be given to the public through that means, such important changes may be necessary as to require recomposition."

The speaker has the advantage over the writer in two ways. He is permitted greater latitude and more repetition. He may interpret his meaning not only by words but by intonations, gesticulations, and changes of facial expression. His main disadvantage is that he must make his meaning apparent at once. He must try not only to communicate to the audience but also to interpret as well.

One of the primary differences is that one style is intended for the eye and the other for the ear. A reader has time to ponder, reread, and look up words if necessary; a hearer must understand the message as it comes or not at all. A reader may proceed at his own pace; a listener goes at the pace of the speaker. If writing does not proceed in linear style, a reader gets bored; but if a speaker avoids repetition, his listener gets lost if concentration is broken even for a moment.

In written style the sentences are longer. In written style more of the sentences are complex in form, whereas in oral style more use is made of the compound sentence.

Repetition is more characteristic of oral than of written style, the reason for this being that when a matter has been recorded the reader may go back to it and check. In oral address it can only be checked if the speaker repeats it. One of the most common means of emphasis is by repetition. Repetition may be an exact duplication of an idea or it may be a restatement. Repetition must be varied by changing the language slightly. This may be accomplished by using stories, by making comparisons, and by applying figures of speech.

VIVIDNESS OF STYLE

Clarity of language allows you to secure understanding; vividness of language allows you to arouse and sustain interest in what you are saying.

Literally, vividness means creating pictures or evoking lifelike mental images. A visual aid allows the audience to see details; vividness allows an audience to picture the details in their imaginations. This depends first of all on the choice of words, and second upon the arrangement of them. The wise use of connectives and special attention to the relationship of qualifying phrases to each other also help. The speaker should try to put himself in the place of the listener and then use words familiar to his listeners.

Likewise his metaphors should be drawn from objects that are familiar to his hearers. Figures of speech use words out of their literal sense to suggest an image or a comparison. They add color and interest to language. Their effective use depends upon originality, vividness, and relevancy to the implied thought. His relative pronouns must be close to their antecedents.

The use of image-producing words is an important feature of oral discourse. It is wise to give special attention to details.

Visual imagery is strengthened by mentioning size, shape, color, movement, and relative position.

Auditory imagery is clarified by noting the pitch, volume, rhythm, quality, and duration.

Gustatory imagery is most easily created by comparison with objects you remember tasting, rather than by the mere use of adjectives. In enhancing the olfactory imagery, it is well to mention not only the odor itself, but also the object producing the odor.

Tactual imagery is based upon the various types of sensation we get from the skin when it is touched. One should describe the shape, texture, pressure, and heat.

Kinesthetic imagery involves reference to muscle strain and movement.

Organic imagery deals with one's present condition, such as hunger or dizziness.

SUMMARY OF STYLE

The acquirement of a good style is largely an unconscious process. Some general helps, however, can be given. There are great advantages in the use of a scriptural style. It is profitable to read the

English Bible audibly as a means of improving one's style. To be steeped in the world of biblical imagery is the key to moving people's hearts. A preacher's growth is tied to reading and reflecting on the Scriptures, not only as a source of faith, but as a study of the language. This helps him to experience how God speaks to us.

General suggestions for improvement of style might include the reading of history for perspective, philosophy for depth, science for objectivity, and current literature to maintain close contact with life.

The preacher will be able to improve his style as he learns more about the people to whom he is to speak. He should be interested in the size of the audience, its cultural climate, the economic status, and the educational level.

There is no absolute ideal of speaking style. Every preacher's rhetorical method must of necessity be his own. It must be natural. This natural style can be cultivated. The good qualities can be improved and the poor ones overcome. Good speaking style will leave the impression that it is produced with ease and with a limited amount of effort. Actually, however, it probably will be the product of constant work and polishing. It will be the preacher's hope that his sermonic style will not only bestow charm upon his subject and authority upon himself as speaker, but more especially that it will bring glory to the God in whose name he speaks.

CLARIFICATION IN SERMONIC ILLUSTRATIONS

The preacher is the man whose calling it is to create forms out of the most precious material which this earth provides. His material is the everlasting gospel, his tools are his full powers of thought and imagination, his object is to create a form which shall be the best possible to convey to other minds and imaginations the glory and beauty of that which he is seeking to portray. Possibly no conception of the preacher's task is greater than that which sets it forth as the work of the creative artist. (F. W. Dillistone, *The Significance of the Cross* [Philadelphia: Westminster, 1944], p. 180)

DEFINITION OF ILLUSTRATIONS

Methodist Bishop H. A. Boaz summarized his theory of effective preaching thus: the preacher should do three things with each point in the sermon: make the point, illustrate it, and apply it. All homileticians agree that this is an ideal combination and sequence. For now, we focus on illustrations.

Perhaps the most important, yet most misused, of the functional elements of a sermon is the illustrations. The illustration is a way to visualize the truth we seek to present. Today, more than ever before, visualizing the truth is crucial to the success of the ser-

mon. People live in a highly visual age. That leads them to expect
this visualization of your message. The illustration must provide the
listener with a verbal picture of the desired truth.

An illustration that requires explanation is worthless. A lamp
should do its own work. I have seen illustrations that were like
ornate table lamps, calling attention to themselves. Good illustrations are like street lamps, scarcely noticed, but throwing floods of
light upon the road. Ornamental lamps will be of little or no use to
you. Honest street lamps will serve your purpose at every turning.[3]

PURPOSES OF ILLUSTRATIONS

It is generally agreed that the four basic purposes of illustrations are: to adorn, to make interesting, to make impressive, and to
make clear. Wakening attention, fixing truth in memory, making truth
vivid, convincing where logic would not, and maintaining freshness,
might also be added to the list. Homileticians have also listed the
enforcement of truth, the arousing of feeling, completing an idea, persuading to action, approving of a point, making truth attractive, providing accuracy, and challenging the thought processes.

Illuminate and clarify. It is apparent that the illustration is the
means used by the sermonizer to illuminate and clarify the logic
and reason of the sermon ideas. Art critic John Ruskin once said,
"The greatest thing a human soul ever does in this world is to 'see'
something, and tell what he 'saw' in a plain way. Hundreds of people
can talk for one who thinks, but thousands can think for one who
can see. To see clearly is poetry, prophecy, religion—all in one."[4]

William Evans says that "the work of the preacher is to make
men first see things, then feel them, then act upon them. If the first
result is not gained the others will fail, while often if the first is
gained, the other two will go."[5] The preacher through the use of
illustrations must make people see things.

Psychology informs us that knowledge is obtained through our
five senses in about the following ratios: sight, 85 percent; hearing,
10 percent; touch, 2 percent; smell, $1^1/2$ percent; and taste, $1^1/2$ percent. If this ratio is essentially true of rhetorical elements, the importance of illustrations that help people "see" should be obvious.
Sermon illustrations are mental pictures that foster knowledge
through inner sight.

Andrew Blackwood declares that the purpose of the illustration is to "make facts shine." Clarification of a subject is a purpose
for illustrations closely akin to illumination.

Good illustrations make truth vivid, and vividness is one of the
most desirable qualities of speech. John Edwards defines
"illustration" as "the art of brightening discourse; of letting in the

light upon our arguments and exhortations."[6] Broadus, in giving the etymology of the word, says that to illustrate . . . is to throw light (or lustre) upon a subject."[7] The second edition of Webster's *New International Unabridged Dictionary* defines "illustration" as "to enlighten mentally," "to illuminate, to set in clear light, to encircle with luster, light, to explain and adorn by pictures." These three definitions make clear that illustration is to illuminate and to make clear one's logic and reason in the sermon.

There should be enough illustration in each sermon to give it luster. The illustration is never to be regarded as an end in itself; it shines for the sake of something beyond. Arguments are the pillars of a discourse, while illustrations are the windows that let in the light. A sermon without illustrations is like a house without windows. A sermon with trivial or pathetic illustrations is worse: it is like a house with broken windows and the holes stuffed with rags and straw.[8] One good illustration carefully done is worth ten ordinary ones carelessly done.

Henry Ward Beecher has said,

> An illustration is a window in an argument, and lets in the light. You may reason without an illustration; but where you are employing a process of pure reasoning and have arrived at a conclusion, if you can then by an illustration flash back light upon what you have said, you will bring into the minds of your audience a realization of your argument that they cannot get in any other way. I have seen an audience, time and again, follow an argument, doubtfully, laboriously, almost suspiciously, and look at one another, as much as to say "Is he going right?"—until the place is arrived at, where the speaker says, "It is like—" and then they listen eagerly for what it is like; and when some apt illustration is thrown out before them there is a sense of relief, as though they said, "Yes, he is right."[9]

Make truth contemporary. In addition to throwing light upon the ideas of the sermon, an illustration should also bridge the gap between the abstract truth of a sermon concept and the concrete application to a life situation. An illustration should incarnate eternal truth in a contemporary situation so that even the youngest in the congregation can feel it is meaningful. John Wesley's advice to his preachers was full of sound sense as he quoted from the words of Aristotle: "Though you think with the learned, you must speak with the common people." Illustrations, then, should make a message practical.

Heighten rhetorical effect. Furthermore, the purpose of illustration is not merely to make the truth clear, but to heighten its nobility and glory. Illustrations give wings to speech so that it may rise above the level of abstraction to that of objectivity. Good illustrations lift the sermon into the heavenlies.

Captivate audience interest. A primary purpose of illustrations is to obtain and hold interest. The right illustration at the beginning of a message may serve to establish rapport with the audience. Beecher used to say that if the illustrations of a sermon were changed, a preacher could repeat any sermon he had preached six months before and no one would recognize it.

As emphasized earlier, the truth shines through the windows of illustrations. "Logic may lay the foundation and build the walls, but illustrations are the windows to let light in."[10] Few people would care to live in houses without windows; even so, few audiences care to hear sermons that lack illustrations. Illustrations are needed in sermons to make a more permanent impression for the truth and to explain a point. Illustrations are used to attract or to arouse attention and to kindle emotional response.

An instance of George Whitefield's power to grip an audience through description and imagination is the following story. He was preaching one day at his tabernacle, and Chesterfield, sitting in Lady Huntingdon's pew, heard him liken a sinner to a blind beggar passing along a dangerous road near a cliff. The beggar's little dog ran away, and he was left alone to probe the perilous path with his iron-shop staff. Finally, he groped to the edge of the precipice and dropped his staff into the abyss. Unaware of his danger, the blind man stooped down to retrieve his staff. Whitefield's description was so graphic that Chesterfield leaped to his feet, crying out, "Great God! He's gone!"

Other purposes. Illustrations tend to rest the audience from close attention and to relax them when the speaker has been particularly intense or abstract.

A preacher may speak indirectly through his illustrations when it would not be wise to speak directly.

KINDS OF ILLUSTRATIONS

Sermon illustrations are usually divided into two kinds—biblical and secular. Within these two kinds of illustrations are a number of different types, ranging from the complete story to the short statement.

In the builder's trade is found an unbelievably large number of window patterns, and new ones are being designed continually. For bank, church, home, school, or factory there are different makes, and for each of these are innumerable varieties from which to select. So it is for the preacher choosing illustrations for particular kinds of sermons.

Words. An illustration may consist of just one striking and picturesque word. One word, concrete in nature and well placed in the sentence, will create a picture of that which the preacher wishes to express. R. G. Lee speaks of a "cross swaying in the darkness with a white, blood-splotched, naked body upon it." Here mere adjectives, "white," "blood-splotched," and "naked," paint an entire portrait.

Phrases. Illustrations may consist of striking and unusual combinations of words. Dawson C. Bryan cites from a *Reader's Digest* column entitled "Toward a More Picturesque Speech," some examples of unusual word combinations: "red-haired autumn," "the day snailed by," "the wrinkled half of my life," "the bells and clocks of the town were discussing midnight," "abrupt as a slammed door," "irrevocable as a haircut," and "as involved as spaghetti."

Stories. The story type of illustration presents truth in action. It captures interest, relieves tension, and applies the truth. The structure of a story is of importance in enabling the listener to progress mentally in its presentation of truth. It progresses from the introduction and the action to the climax and its conclusion.

The introduction must be short and concise in answering the questions who, when, and where. The action follows a sequence of events leading to a climax of interest on the part of the listener. The conclusion of the story relieves the tension of the climax and enables the message of the illustration to shine through.

Parables. The parable is more than just a story used to illuminate a principle or truth. As used by Jesus in the New Testament, the parable contained allegory, simile, and metaphor. The parables He used revealed truth, stimulated thought, and won the attention of the listeners by the combination of simplicity of expression and the presentation of profound truth.

Most preachers have difficulties in inventing new parables for use as illustrations. It is usually best to use Christ's parables in the illustration of scriptural truth.

Allegories. An allegory portrays a spiritual truth in figurative language. It employs a symbol or an emblem to suggest the meaning. Often virtues, vices, and various moral qualities are personalized in the allegory. Examples of this use of the allegory are seen in John Bunyan's *Pilgrim's Progress.* Mr. Obstinate, Mr. Greatheart, and others portray various moral qualities.

Myths, fables, and folklore. Tales of fiction often contain moral truth. This is often accomplished by attributing reason and verbal skills to trees, birds, beasts, and other elements. Books on mythology and folklore, such as *Aesop's Fables,* should be used for this type of illustration.

Object lessons. Books on object lessons are usually available at Christian bookstores. The object lesson is valuable for children's sermons or for dealing with a believing audience.

Readily accessible materials may be used for object lessons and are effective visual aids. Such devices catch and hold the attention of the eye while the truth is explained.

Poems or hymns. Often a poem or hymn brings into focus an idea or truth difficult to express in prose. But exercise care in the selection of poems that are lengthy or wordy. You should not read poetry or hymns since that usually detracts from their effectiveness. If the material is worth quoting, it should be worth memorizing. Hymns are especially valuable in this regard because they are usually more familiar and direct.

Proverbs. Proverbs, when used briefly and forcibly, are excellent illustrations. The characteristics of the proverb as a short, pointed, witty, and practical saying usually help the preacher condense his idea into a few words. Too many proverbs are difficult for the listener to organize and remember; therefore, be selective in their use.

Quotations. The use of a quotation to offer an opinion or provide support for an idea is helpful in the establishment of a position. Use quotations sparingly when necessary, due to controversy in the minds of the audience. Sermons are not helped by having many direct quotations. Usually a paraphrase is adequate.

Analogies, similes, and metaphors. These figures of speech are used as illustrations to express similarities between different things. The metaphor is a common type of figurative language in which a word or phrase literally denotes one kind of object or idea in place of another by way of suggesting a likeness or analogy between them (e.g., the ship plows the sea). The simile is a figure of speech directly expressing a resemblance (by using "like" or "as") in one or more points of comparison.

Beecher was definitely a metaphorical preacher. So was Thomas Talmage. One of the most famous speeches in American oratory was William Jennings Bryan's at the 1896 Democratic Convention, when he brought delegates cheering to their feet with his celebrated metaphor borrowed from the crucifixion, "You shall not press down upon the brow of labor this crown of thorns. You shall not crucify mankind upon a cross of gold."

> Spurgeon has said concerning metaphorical illustrations: "They should not be too numerous. . . . Some men seem never to have enough of metaphors; each one of their sentences must be a flower. They compass sea and land to find a fresh piece of colored glass for their windows. . . . Flowers upon the table at a banquet are well

enough; but as nobody can live on banquets, they will become objects of contempt if they are set before us in lieu of substantial viands. The difference between a little salt with your meat and being compelled to empty the salt cellar is clear to all." Here we have four metaphors in immediate succession to illustrate the principle of moderation in the use of metaphor—an admirable example of the violation of a principle in the very act of enforcing.[12]

In the use of figures of speech the greatest example is our Lord Himself. He was always saying, "The kingdom of heaven is like unto—" the seed sown in the ground, the wheat and the tares, the plowman who came upon the hidden treasure, the mustard tree, the women who put the leaven in the lump, the woman who searched for the lost coin, the merchant who bought the goodly pearl, the lilies of the field, the birds of the air, and the hen covering her chickens with her wing.

Hyperboles. The hyperbole is an obvious exaggeration or extravagant statement used to highlight the intensity of the truth. Often its use makes a deep and lasting impression on the mind of the listener.

Paradoxes. The statement of a proposition that at first seems to contradict itself is a paradox. It is often used to draw attention to the truth as Paul does in 2 Corinthians 6:9-10: "as unknown, and yet well-known, as dying yet behold, we live; as punished yet not put to death, as sorrowful, yet always rejoicing, as poor, yet making many rich, as having nothing yet possessing all things."

Contrasts. The examination of differences is an excellent way to heighten or demonstrate the validity of an idea. Often the opposite idea, when expressed, will make the thought you wish to convey stand out in the listener's mind.

SOURCES OF ILLUSTRATIONS

The Bible. This source should not be overlooked in your search for illustrations. The Bible is a rich storehouse of illustration of man's religious experience and when used as a source for illustrations, accomplishes a twofold purpose. First, it increases the listeners' and the preachers' knowledge of the Bible. Second, it provides biblical authority for the concept or idea and its application. Do not neglect the Bible as a source of sermon illustrations.

Pastoral experience and personal observation. These are rich sources of illustrative material. However, care must be taken in using pastoral experience and personal observation. Often what the pastor discovers and observes is confidential and should not appear in his sermons. However, many of these experiences are

down-to-earth and life-related, and they provide for instant application on the part of the listener.

Biography and autobiography. Such autobiographical classics
as *The Journal of John Wesley, The Confessions of St. Augustine, The
Autobiography of Mark Rutherford,* and Albert Schweitzer's *Out of
My Life and Thought* abound in illustrative material.[12] F. W. Boreham
was a master in the use of biographical illustrations.

Literature. Charles Dickens' tales are well suited for use by the
preacher, for Dickens, too, was a great preacher. In *A Tale of Two
Cities* Dickens describes Sydney Carton going up to his lonely lodg-
ing and weeping on his unmade bed over his wasted life and lost
opportunities.

The tales of Victor Hugo abound in powerful illustrations for
the preacher. In *Toilers of the Seas* there is a great passage on retri-
bution.

Nathaniel Hawthorne was a great moralist, and almost all of his
works are forceful sermonettes. Most familiar, perhaps, is *The Scarlet Letter,* showing how sin always scars the heart.

Poems. These also may be used as illustrations. In poetry, truth
can be expressed in beautiful and imaginative language, concisely
and effectively phrased. Using poetry to illustrate will not only help
to illuminate but will add beauty to the truth expressed.

Nature. Henry Ward Beecher and Hugh Macmillan were fond
of illustrations from nature and knew far more about seeds, grasses,
flowers, and plants than the average man. Some of Beecher's most
effective illustrations are in his sermon "The Ages to Come."

Children and family life. The situations, humorous and serious,
that arise in the lives of families and their children often provide
excellent illustrations. The temperament, habits, and actions of children are readily adaptable to various aspects of truth. We should
become familiar with the activities of the family at home, at school,
at work, at play, and at church.

History. The events and activities of history—ancient,
medieval, and modern—provide you with interesting illustrations.
Many events lend themselves to explanation and interpretation for
sermon purposes. Remember to keep the illustration factual, but
brief and interesting, to assist the congregation in reliving it.

Missions. In an attempt to broaden the horizons of outreach
and acquaint the congregation with current mission activities, illustrations of truth from this area should be used.

Your contacts with missionaries, their boards, and the situations that develop in their attempts to extend the outreach of the
church provide stimulating illustrations of truth in action.

Art and architecture. Oftentimes art and architecture symbolize certain spiritual truths. Keep your illustrations brief and free from the appearance of "show" to impress others.

Imagination. When all else fails, use your power of imagination. Do not attempt to hide the use of imagination from the listeners, but inform them of its source. Allow them to employ their power of imagination.

Imagination is the picture-making faculty of the mind. It must always be under the control of reality and stay with facts. It sees what is, what might have been, what can now be, and what might be. Imagination is vital to the preacher in two ways: it can help him project himself into the experiences of others (empathy); and it can help put truth into images people can see and feel—thus turning the ear into an eye. The force of the imagination can be communicated by using well chosen details, sound judgment, good taste, and a keen sense of responsibility. Excessive and exaggerated use of imagination is defeating. Imagination can be used effectively in constructing and inventing, in picturing and illustrating, in reproducing the past and giving vividness to today.

USES OF ILLUSTRATIONS

Recommended usage. The preacher should vary his techniques in using illustrations. He will normally have at least one major illustration for each main point. While it is good to follow Aristotle's advice of using one major illustration for every main point, this should not be the unalterable pattern.

The type of sermon may be one factor that will prompt him to alter the number of illustrations. Biographical, parabolic, and historical messages do not need as many illustrations as do doctrinal messages.

As a general rule, it is wise for the preacher not to talk about illustrating but just to illustrate.

Illustrations should be carefully planned and carefully prepared for the most effective use. They should be varied in types and sources.

"Illustrate your sermons," says Dr. John A. Kern, "but do not indulge the weakness of sermonizing your illustrations."

Webb B. Garrison discusses the criteria of a "good" illustration. "An illustration should be understandable, pertinent, and applicable to the point being illustrated. It must be commensurate with the theme."[13]

Much advice is offered by the homiletical writers as to how the sermonizer should select and present illustrative material.

It should be easily understood.
It should be truthful.
It should be subservient to the main thought.
It should be brief, with only one point.
Use Bible illustrations freely.
Use old illustrations sparingly.
Use illustrations that are clear, concise, and pointed.
Use only reasonable illustrations.
Let the occasion, character of audience, and style of message determine the illustration.
Scatter the illustrations throughout the sermon.
Limit the number of humorous illustrations.
Short illustrations are better than long ones.
Be sure that you know your illustrations.
Be sure the facts of the illustration are scrupulously accurate; avoid exaggeration.
Remember that some messages only require figures of speech as illustrations.
Don't use two illustrations for one truth.
Don't use two illustrations from one area of interest.
Don't apologize for using personal illustrations.
Don't use illustrations that need to be explained.
Avoid the first person pronoun in the illustration.
An illustration should not be used just for itself.
Quote poetry sparingly.
Use only short quotations of poetry.

Use no illustration that you do not thoroughly understand. Don't hurry away from an illustration, and do not use too many illustrations. Cultivate your powers of narration and description, and make use of a wide diversity of illustrative material. Be sure that the illustrations you use do not contradict what your own life teaches.

The character of the sermon determines the length of the illustrations. The illustrations in doctrinal sermons should be shorter than those in evangelistic preaching.

An illustration must be long enough to bring out the point in a clear, well-defined impression and to catch the attention firmly.

Different congregations require different illustrations as regards length. A cultured audience can receive most in a few words. Remember that, in the long run, very long illustrations take the mind too long away from the main trend of the sermon.

It is preferable to err on the side of making the illustration too brief. You will get fixed attention with the shorter illustration. Better be short than sorry. Verbosity is always dangerous and never more so than in using illustrations.

Disapproved usage. A sermon is not a shish kebab skewer, alternating biblical meat with interesting anecdotes. If an illustration does not enlighten, it distracts, and an irrelevant illustration is worse than none. Failing to clarify, it creates confusion.

Avoid illustrations that reveal a lack of good taste or good judgment on the part of the user. Eliminate the highly improbable and all illustrations that create a laugh about any passage of Scripture. Eliminate all humor about hell and that which mocks human disabilities such as stammering. Be careful not to use illustrations that are so forceful and dramatic that they call attention to themselves rather than to the point you are making. Avoid illustrations that duplicate a point already sufficiently illustrated, those that merely pad out a sermon, without adding any strength. Eliminate local incidents involving known individuals that discredit them. Illustrations should be omitted that might offend members of various ethnic and minority groups.

MODELS OF ILLUSTRATIONS

Notable preachers. Most of the great preachers have been adept in their use of illustrations. J. W. Etter says:

> The most successful preachers . . . such as Chrysostom, Evans, Chalmers, Guthrie, Todd, Beecher, Spurgeon, Talmadge, Moody . . . have shown the force of illustrations in preaching. But the use of illustrations in expressing and enforcing religious truths has a higher sanction. Christ's public discourses abounded with numerous parables, figures, and illustrations drawn from familiar objects. His *Sermon on the Mount* is illustrated by salt, the candle, the city on the hill, the fowl of the air, the lilies of the field, the house built on the sand; and scarcely ever did He speak without a parable or illustration.[14]

Learn from good preaching examples who were proficient in the use of illustrative material. George W. Truett was outstanding in the use of illustrative stories from his own personal experience. John Henry Jowett was an artist in the use of language and always had his illustrations skillfully adjusted to his message in the fewest possible words.

Thomas Guthrie was a master in the use of illustrations at the beginning of a sermon. In his sermon "The Sins and Sorrows of the City" he describes what a man might see in the ocean under his boat on a quiet day.

> The standing stumps of trees and the mouldering vestiges of a forest where once the wild cat prowled and the birds of heaven, singing their

loves, had nestled and nursed their young. . . .[The same phenomenon could be seen in our great cities.] Not a single house or block of houses, but whole streets . . . had been engulfed. A flood of ignorance and misery and sin now breaks and roars above the top of their highest tenements.[15]

Charles Haddon Spurgeon of the nineteenth century still casts his shadow over the twentieth.

It was not merely theology he preached; his truth was often embodied in a tale, and the arrow of his appeal was winged with a wise and witty saying. His wide and keen observation of life, his varied reading, supplied him with abundant illustrations of the doctrine he set forth. His preaching was natural, without pulpit affectation; he talked with fullness and freshness of thought. He knew how to make even an ordinary subject interesting by unhackneyed exposition and illustration.[16]

Frederick W. Robertson's sensitive and powerful sermons had an irresistible appeal. "They are based on a constant and minute study of the Scriptures; they breathe the spirit of intense devoutness; they are most searching in their scrutiny of the experience and character of men; they are illumined by illustrations drawn from varied and accurate study; . . . and the center is in Christ the Savior."[17]

Henry Ward Beecher was a man of vivid imagination and intense passion, extraordinarily dramatic. "He was constantly studying the Bible, the world around him, the men he met, reading, observing, meditating with one object, to gather material for his pulpit."[18]

The pre-eminent preacher of the last century, and possibly of the American pulpit, was Phillips Brooks. He gave untiring labor to sermon preparation. "He was a very hard worker, a very diligent student, reading widely 'science literature, biography, history, poetry'; but the one thing he did was to preach, using all else for this end."[19]

Jesus Christ. Christ used illustrations extensively. He used them to silence objectors, to explain the laws of His kingdom and their operation, to explain the truth and the working of it, to unfold the spiritual life and development to the believer, or to make some other point. Sometimes the whole discourse is woven around one illustration. The language was carefully chosen. Sometimes He made the application, and sometimes He left it to the hearers. Sometimes He told an illustration that had an application that none of His hearers would get, knowing that those who were interested would ask Him to clarify the intended meaning. By the number and variety of His illustrations, the Lord Jesus becomes the preacher's best model.

The paradoxical thing about a system to retain sermon illustrations is that, despite its necessity, it is rarely satisfactory. The preacher must have some system of storage and retrieval, but he should determine ahead of time that the one he chooses will work for him.

George Buttrick, whose picturesque style and vivid illustrations are unique, was asked how he kept his materials. He gave this surprising answer: "I am fortunate enough to possess a photographic memory. Once having seen anything in print, I can usually recall it verbatim."[20]

O. W. McCall says, "I mark the books that I read so that I may find again what I want should my memory indicate to me that what I want is somewhere in the book."[21]

Many ministers, like Phillips Brooks, keep a notebook in which they record a suggestion or a more elaborate outline of the incident. This notebook should also contain illustrations that are found outside of books, arising from pastoral visiting, travel, nature, and the imagination.[22]

The most complete system of which I know is that of Bishop George Craig Stewart. Let him tell how he used it in sermon preparation.

> I make a rough brief outline to secure sound structural treatment. The second stage is to take that outline and elaborate it. In doing this I utilize the index system which for nearly thirty years I have developed. Every book as it is read, and this means several books a week, bears upon its last page or two a topical index created as I go along. When the book is read my secretary indexes these topics on cards which now number a great many thousand. All magazines are read and marked for clipping and filing. When, therefore, I come to the elaboration of my outline, such books and clippings as may be involved in the subjects which develop in the outline are carefully searched for allusive and illustrative materials.[23]

Stephen S. Wise of New York City, one of the world's outstanding rabbis, tells of his method of preparation as follows:

> As for preparing a sermon and speech, I have twenty to thirty and perhaps even more envelopes on my desk containing material on things about which some day I am going to preach. As I read and think, I make memoranda and put the items into different envelopes. A great deal of this material I shall never use, but again it is a case of a sermon ripening rather than being delivered, and prepared ad hoc or delivered impromptu, save for a few days preparation.[24]

There are several filing systems that might be used to file illustrative material.

The Efficiency Filing System, by L. R. Elliott, describes such a system for organizing the preacher's library and a simple system for indexing the material of the library and other material. It is an easily used filing system.[25]

The Eureka Filing System is an adaptation of the *Wilson Index System.* It provides for the filing and indexing of loose materials, the indexing of books and periodicals, and the filing and indexing of sermons under subjects and texts. It is relatively simple and easily used.[26]

Baker's Textual and Topical Filing System, by Neal Punt, provides for the organizing of material in the preacher's library and filing cabinet by means of one complete index. The material is indexed under topics and texts.[27]

The Rossin-Dewey System outlines a method for filing clippings, tracts, notes, and sermons by the use of the Dewey Decimal system of classification.[28]

A Word Fitly Spoken, by Robert J. Hastins, describes nearly forty sources of illustrations and gives examples. It also offers a system for classifying and filing them.[29]

CLARIFICATION IN SERMONIC APPLICATIONS

The whole application of the Word of God to the present day must follow the lines and reproduce the characteristic features of the text, so that the text may without difficulty be recognized from the application. This is demanded by the dignity of the text as well as by the homiletic conscience of the preacher. The homilete must so completely assimilate this principle that it will become his second nature, and that he will be unable to act contrary to it because his conscience will not permit. (J. M. Reu, *Homiletics: Manual of the Theory and Practice of Preaching* [Grand Rapids: Baker, 1967], p. 362)

What is the difference between an expository *lesson* and an expository *sermon*? The main goal of an expository lesson is the impartation of information. Its primary direction is toward the mind. It aims at a change of belief on the part of the hearer, whereas the expository sermon aims not only at a change of belief, but also of behavior.

The expository sermon includes information, but it also includes an abundance of application. Some have said that preaching begins where the application begins. The primary direction of the expository sermon is toward the will. The application highlights for the listener his relationship to the proposition of the sermon by focusing on the responsibility toward it and how that responsibility can be carried out in daily living.

CLASSIFYING THE APPLICATIONS

Applications should be present in a sermon because many of those in the audience lack the spiritual, homiletical, hermeneutical, and mental skills necessary to apply the truth of the sermon to themselves. Many lack the will to apply the truth of the sermon to sensitive areas in their lives. Applications help the audience see the relevance of the truth and what the truth has to do with them. It also helps make clear what they ought to do in response to the truth.

The purpose of the application will vary with the purpose of the sermon. If the sermon is directed toward unbelievers and has for its purpose the conversion of the individual through the ministry of the Holy Spirit, then the application will be one of challenge for an initial faith or evangelical response. If the sermon is directed toward believers and has for its purpose the healing of the individual life, then the application will be one of challenge to accept and respond to the proposed cure. This might be termed the therapeutic response. In a sermon we are not interested in conveying information that stops short of bringing about a change of attitude and activity. This might be termed the didactic response.

DIFFERENTIATING THE APPLICATIONS

Formal or functional applications? The terms *application* and *conclusion* are not synonymous. Application is a moral or spiritual term which specifies the use to which the message is directed. Conclusion is a rhetorical term denoting the closing portion of an address. Application is a functional element of the sermon, but the conclusion is a formal element within the sermon. Other formal elements would include such items as the introduction, proposition, main points, and sub-points. These are settled as to location within the sermonic framework. Functional elements such as the application may make an appearance at many points within the sermon. Functional elements are active in nature and are part of the formal factors.

Compact or continued applications? When the application appears only in the conclusion of a sermon, it is called *compact* application since it is centered in one location at the close of the message. When the application appears at many points throughout the sermon, it is referred to as a *continued* application. One of the

chief excellencies of the Puritan preachers was found in their continued or running applications.

The preacher may make use of what is called *divisional* applications. This refers to the applications that come at the close of
each major division within the message. The conclusion of such a
message might be a recapitulation of the divisional applications.
Divisional applications are a subspecies of the continued application.

American preaching in past years has been characterized by
compact applications. The changes in listeners and the listening
context would appear to suggest that this practice should be
changed and that the continued applications should be employed.

When the application is reserved for the conclusion, it may
then be stale and lifeless. The congregation has been forced to wait
too long to see the practical import of the message for their daily
living. They may also have made preliminary applications on their
own so that the applications within the conclusion are mere repetitions.

On the other hand, there is a danger to be encountered in the
use of the continued application. It may result in having no single
strong impression within the sermon.

UNDERSTANDING OF APPLICATIONS

Timeless. An effective, functional element of application within
a message depends partly upon the nature of the formal elements.
When the formal element is timeless in nature, then it will be easy
to see and share its application. Proper names within formal elements of the sermon, other than the names of deity, tie that element
to yesterday. These proper names of people and places should
therefore be omitted in the title, subject, theme, proposition, and
main points. These items should be worded in a way that they
would have relevance for Bible days and for the present time as
well.

By being timeless we refer to an item in a form that shows its
relationship not only to yesterday but also to today and tomorrow.

A timeless application can be expected since Scripture is the
Word of the changeless God and since it was directed to mankind
whose heart remains the same.

If we are to apply the message to the lives of the listeners, then
the message must be based upon the timeless theme of the passage
of Scripture. What was the main thrust of that passage of Scripture
when it was first presented? Did it deal with a problem, need, or
issue that is also relevant to life in today's world? The theme must

be anchored in God's timeless Word and also in God's world. When we preach upon a theme, the listeners have a right to ask, "So what?" Some messages may be detached almost completely from life as it really is. The messages may be aimed at the Corinthians, and there may be no Corinthians present.

Personal. The speaker may employ direct forms of application within the message. He may give a specific exhortation accompanied by specific steps to take in making the exhortation a reality in daily living.

The application of a sermon must always be personal. It must also include means and methods. An exhortation to do something is not enough. This must be followed with an outlined practical procedure for doing it. The application should deal with particulars. Many messages fail because the preacher has not made plain to himself precisely what he is urging his listeners to be and to do. The preacher must determine the focus of the application from the beginning of his message. The application is planned even during the preparation.

The speaker may make use of a series of rhetorical questions such as, "What is your response to this message?" "What will you do about this suggestion?" This suggestive type of application was often used by Jesus. He should then follow the rhetorical question or questions with some possible optional responses and challenge them to act upon one. If the speaker were to merely list the options then he would have an *indirect* application. His emphasis upon the acceptance of one specific option makes it *direct.*

The speaker may employ indirect application by employing a narrative. The point of the story centers in the application that is desired as a response to the message. The speaker refrains at that point from "moralizing" and leaves the listener to see the point and act upon it.

DISCOVERING THE APPLICATIONS

The application is in the text and is discovered there. The text is chosen because the preacher sees the application in it, and the subject of the text is so announced by the preacher that it contains the application in its initial form. Proper handling of the text can bring out the correct application whereas improper handling may obscure the obvious application.

The timeless truth, once discovered in the text, must be set forth in all naturalness so that the application will grow by an inner necessity out of the text and will be nothing else than the organic unfolding of the text.

The main thought in the text will be the main thought in the application. What is not found in the text will not be found in the application.

The inferential method. In this case the speaker looks at the formal sermonic item before him and asks, "What inferences of a practical nature can be drawn from this item as stated?" This method is especially useful when the item is of an abstract nature. The speaker must beware of reading into an item that which cannot logically be inferred from it.

The inferences must not only be tested by human logic, but also by the scriptural content. The inferences drawn from the item must be in accord with the total testimony of Scripture since the Bible is our rule of faith and practice. The preacher should be honest with his listeners. He should share with them whether the inferences being drawn are known by him to be logical and scripturally valid or whether they are mere speculations on his part.

The interrogation method. Three progressive questions can serve as guides in forming an effective application.

What does this item mean?
How does this item relate to the area of activity of my audience in general?
How does this item relate to specific types of individuals within the audience?

Someone has suggested that the preacher should put a sign over his study desk with one word upon it, "How?"

How can this fact be developed?
How can this fact be avoided?
How can this fact be put into practice?
How can this fact be accomplished?

These and other similar questions applied to formal homiletical items within the message will help to pry out the application.

ADAPTING THE APPLICATIONS

The adaptation of the applications will be governed by the areas of major concern represented among the listeners. These may include such major concerns as family, government, business, church life, personal adjustment, and social relationships.

Some ministers sharpen their audience awareness by keeping a card on their desks with the names of six or as many as twelve parishioners on it. For example, the names of a six-year-old boy, a fourteen-year-old boy, a fourteen-year-old girl, a teenage couple, a young married couple, parents of a young family, a business man, a widow, and a retired couple. It should also be remembered, however, that the preacher must never single out a person by name or give details so that an audience can determine to whom the preacher is referring. Audience analysis can be pursued through the examination of membership records, interest inventories, questionnaires, and testing.

The exposure to the congregation while engaged in pastoral visitation will help in analyzing their attitudes, attachments, and activities. The preacher keeps asking, "What is my congregation's present state? Where and how far from their present state can they move? At what point does this message touch the lives of people?"

Applications are best stated by the use of the present tense. This will be made easier when the main points of the message are also stated in the present tense. The preacher should write out the applications for the sermon in order that he may give them with clarity and pointedness.

EVALUATING THE APPLICATIONS

Some preachers have found it practical to test applications before the message is given. This can be done by asking family members and associates to evaluate the possible applications you see in a passage. They may comment on their practicality and may also suggest some additional possibilities.

In connection with dialogical preaching some preachers have formed a sermon board in their church, which is composed of about eight members from different walks of life. These meet once each week to examine the passages to be used as bases for the message of the coming Lord's Day. One of the examination points pertains to the search for, and evaluation of, applications for family living.

Some have suggested a short period to be set aside after a message in which the listeners share ways whereby the sermon may be transposed into daily life. This allows the individuals a chance to listen to the applications of others, crystallize their own thinking, and arrive at additional possibilities for application. Applications must be practical. By this we mean that they must be within the immediate reach of the congregation. The preacher must operate within the realm of realism rather than in the realm of idealism.

DEVELOPING THE APPLICATIONS

Applications should be woven into the message in connection with each spiritual truth mentioned. One of the ways of gaining proficiency in this is to make two parallel lists on a sheet of paper. In one the spiritual truth is listed and in the other is listed the possible applications. For practice in developing these applications one could make a list of characteristic human traits and behavior patterns. Beside each of these he could list an appropriate Scripture passage.

A factor that will control the amount of time spent in developing application within the sermon is the complexity of the truth being presented. When an excessive amount of time is necessary to explain the truth being presented then the amount of time for application is limited. It is wise to keep both of these processes within reasonable boundaries.

PERSONALIZING THE APPLICATIONS

Through wording. The language of application should be direct and personal. Few things weaken the application more than unnecessary and indirect words. Of course, it should be characterized by tactfulness and courtesy. Sometimes this will mean that indirect address will be used when the topic of application indicates need for discretion. A list of indefinite words might include such words as *people, someone, a Christian, a church member,* and *mankind.*

However, normally applications should be direct, and this will depend upon nouns and pronouns. The first and second person pronouns make applications direct and personal. There are times when the strong form of the second person "you need to . . ." should be modified by using the first person and saying "we need to . . ." The directness of the application will vary with the amount of personal authority and personal experience behind the preacher's declaration. The directness will also be tempered by the amount of scriptural truth behind the application over against the nonbiblical remarks added by the preacher.

Through example. The application in the preacher's inner life is evident in the spirit and manner of his life and ministry rather than in any specific language he employs to express it. It will be conveyed by his sincerity, earnestness, and fidelity to the Word of God. Before the application can live and move in the souls of the hearers it must burn and glow in the heart of the preacher.

Through explanation. Direct application may be characterized by instruction and by persuasion. It is instructional when it gives a process outlining the method of proceeding from the explanation to implementation in daily life.

Through motivation. Direct application is persuasive when the speaker helps the listener feel the truth and motivates him to action. This persuasible aspect highlights the task of the speaker to renew the inner motives of the listener as well as his will. We should beware of applications that result in outward acts without the proper motivation. Applications should strengthen faith as well as point to outward activities.

Through illustrations. Good illustrative materials help application. The illustration is the picture or photograph that goes along with an abstract idea and serves to assist application. Good illustrations make applications come to life. They clarify the application and arouse interest in it. They enforce the point through indirection, thus allowing the listener to get the point. Illustrative material makes the application concrete so that the listener sees it, thus making it easier to remember. The illustration is not the application, but it does help to clarify the application. The right kind of illustration provides a mental picture in which the hearer actually sees the point of application.

PURSUING THE APPLICATIONS

Despite challenge of doctrine. Some types of biblical material present more of a challenge for application than others. One of these types of material is the *doctrinal.* This by its very nature is loaded with truth content. This means that it is directed basically toward the mind rather than toward the will. The emphasis is upon that which we should believe rather than upon that which we should do. Some doctrines are better taught than preached. The doctrine is not ready for preaching until we can see its practical application for present-day living. Until we have bridged the gap between doctrine and duty, the material should be presented in a class setting rather than in a church service under the heading of a sermon.

Despite challenge of parables. Application for sermons preached on *parables* presents a special challenge because of the hermeneutical problems involved. Some parables are intended to present one main truth. In such a case this one truth is applied to various situations. There are some parables where the details of the parable provide help in guiding the application.

Despite challenge of miracles. Application presents a special challenge in sermons based upon biblical *miracles.* The main problem is centered in discerning the original purpose for the performance of the miracle.

Despite challenge of narratives. When preaching on *historical narrative texts*, we should beware of abstracting the application away from the unique circumstances of the text. The preacher will look for the universal element giving continuity between the event then and life now, but he will not overlook factors of discontinuity that should influence any present response of faith.

Despite challenge of monotony. One of the chief perils of the pulpit in developing application is that of sameness. This may be avoided first of all by directing the applications to different groups of individuals. A second method is to make certain that each application stresses a different item to be developed and a different action to be carried out. A third method is to make certain that the application is geared to the unique emphasis of that particular theme being applied.

Despite challenge of diversity. Preaching audiences not only differ one from the other but also usually include within each one a great diversity of individuals. To give good practical suggestions to such a mixture of human beings is no small task. It calls for growing experience, thoughtful observation, and delicate tact. The preacher must remember that one of the measures of his success in preaching is to be found in the degree in which the application of the sermon is subsequently practiced by the audience.

J. H. Jowett in his book entitled *The Preacher: His Life and Work* says: "Keep in mind at least a dozen men and women, very varied in their natural temperaments, and very dissimilar in their daily circumstances. When I am preparing my work, my mind is constantly glancing around this invisible circle, and I consider how I can so serve the bread of this particular truth as to provide welcome nutriment for all."[30]

NOTES

1. Charles E. Jefferson, *Quiet Hints to Growing Preachers in My Study* (New York: Thomas Y. Crowell, 1901), p. 177.

2. Robert J. McCracken, *The Making of the Sermon* (New York: Harper, 1956), p. 73.

3. J. H. Jowett, *The Preacher: His Life and Work* (New York: Harper, 1912), pp. 140-41.

4. John Ruskin, *Modern Painters,* 5 vols. (London: Smith, Eldon, 1846-60), 3: pt. iv. chap. xvi, 28.

5. William Evans, *How to Prepare Sermons and Gospel Addresses* (Chicago: Moody, 1964), p. 135.

6. John Edwards, *The Art of Illustrating Illustrated* (London: R. Culley, 1909), p. 9.

7. John Broadus, *A Treatise on the Preparation and Delivery of Sermons* (New York: Harper, 1944), p. 213.

8. George A. Buttrick, *Jesus Came Preaching* (Grand Rapids: Baker, 1970), p. 159.

9. B. B. Baxter, *The Heart of the Yale Lectures* (New York: Macmillan, 1947), p. 152.

10. Evans, *How to Prepare Sermons,* p. 137.

11. John A. Kern, *The Ministry to the Congregation* (New York: Jennings & Graham, 1897), p. 226.

12. Brown, Clinard, Northcutt, *Steps to the Sermon,* p. 73.

13. Webb B. Garrison, *The Preacher and His Audience* (Westwood, N. J.: Revell, 1954), pp. 178-83.

14. J. W. Etter, *The Preacher and His Sermon* (Dayton, Ohio: W. J. Shuey, 1883), p. 338.

15. Clarence Macartney, *Great Sermons of the World* (Boston: Stratford, 1926), p. 433.

16. A. E. Garvie, *The Christian Preacher* (New York: Charles Scribner's, 1937), p. 248.

17. Ibid., p. 254.

18. Ibid.

19. Ibid., p. 260.

20. Dawson Bryan, *The Art of Illustrating Sermons* (Nashville: Abingdon-Cokesbury, 1938), p. 153.

21. Joseph Fort Newton, *If I Had Only One Sermon to Prepare* (New York: Harper, 1932), p. 197.

22. Bryan, *The Art of Illustrating Sermons*, p. 155.

23. Newton, *If I Had Only One Sermon to Prepare*, pp. 157-58.

24. Edgar DeWitt Jones, *American Preachers of Today* (Freeport, N.Y.: Books for Libraries, 1921), p. 66.

25. L. R. Elliott, *The Efficiency Filing System* (Nashville: Broadman, 1959), p. 81.

26. Available through the Student Center, Southern Baptist Theological Seminary, Louisville, Kentucky.

27. Neal Punt, *Baker's Textual and Topical Filing System* (Grand Rapids: Baker, 1960).

28. Donald F. Rossin and Palmer Ruschke, *Practical Study Methods for Student and Pastor* (Minneapolis: T. S. Denison, 1956).

29. Robert J. Hastings, *A Word Fitly Spoken* (Nashville: Broadman, 1962).

30. John H. Jowett, *The Preacher, His Life and Work* (New York: George H. Doran, 1912), pp. 135ff.

BIBLIOGRAPHY

CONCERNING SERMONIC STYLE

Adams, Jay E. *Preaching with Purpose.* Grand Rapids: Baker, 1982.

Baird, John E. *Preparing for Platform and Pulpit.* Nashville: Abingdon, 1968.

* Baumann, J. Daniel. *An Introduction to Contemporary Preaching.* Grand Rapids: Baker, 1972.

* Broadus, John Albert. *A Treatise on the Preparation and Delivery of Sermons.* New York: A. C. Armstrong, 1889.

Dadney, Robert Lewis. *Sacred Rhetoric: Lectures on Preaching.* New York: Anson D. F. Randolph, 1870.

* Engel, James. *How Can I Get Them to Listen?* Grand Rapids: Zondervan, 1977.

Garrison, Webb Black. *The Preacher and His Audience.* Westwood, N. J.: Revell, 1954.

* McLaughlin, Raymond W. *Communication for the Church.* Grand Rapids: Zondervan, 1968.

Thonssen, Lester. *Selected Readings in Rhetoric and Public Speaking.* New York: H. W. Wilson, 1942.

CONCERNING SERMONIC ILLUSTRATIONS

* Allee, G. Franklin. *Evangelistic Illustrations for Pulpit and Platform.* Chicago: Moody, 1961.

Barnhouse, Donald Gray. *Let Me Illustrate.* Westwood, N. J.: Revell, 1967.

Breed, David Riddle. *Preparing to Preach.* New York: George H. Doran, 1911.

Bryan, Dawson D. *The Art of Illustrating Sermons.* Nashville: Cokesbury, 1938.

Drakford, John W. *Humor in Preaching.* Grand Rapids: Zondervan; Ministry Resources Library, 1986.

Fisk, Franklin Woodbury. *A Manual of Preaching: Lectures on Homiletics.* New York: A. C. Armstrong, 1895.

* Hostetter, Michael J. *Introducing the Sermon: The Art of Compelling Beginnings.* Grand Rapids: Zondervan, 1986.

Jones, Ilion T. *Principles and Practice of Preaching.* Nashville; Abingdon, 1956.

Kern, John Adam. *The Ministry to the Congregation: Lectures on Homiletics.* New York: Jennings and Graham, 1897.

* MacPherson, Ian. *The Art of Illustrating Sermons.* Nashville: Abingdon, 1964.

Pickering, H. *One Thousand Tales Worth Telling.* London: Pickering & Inglis, n.d.

* Skinner, Craig. *The Teaching Ministry of the Pulpit.* Grand Rapids: Baker, 1973.

Wells, Amos R. *Studies in the Art of Illustration.* New York: Revell, 1903.

CONCERNING SERMONIC APPLICATIONS

Bowie, Walter Russel. *Preaching.* Nashville: Abingdon, 1954.

Breed, David Riddle. *Preparing to Preach.* New York: George H. Doran, 1911.

Broadus, John Albert. *A Treatise on the Preparation and Delivery of Sermons.* New York: A. C. Armstrong, 1889.

* Brown, H. C., Jr. *A Quest for Reformation in Preaching.* Waco, Tex.: Word, 1968.

Caemmerer, Richard R. *Preaching for the Church.* St. Louis: Concordia, 1959.

Johnson, Herrick. *The Ideal Ministry.* New York: Revell, 1908.

* Vines, Jerry. *A Practical Guide to Sermon Preparation.* Chicago: Moody, 1985.

6

BIBLICAL PREACHING AND LIFE-SITUATION PREACHING

The advantage of preparing a sermon with the actual needs of our people in mind is [that] . . . we are dealing with the daily discouragements, the constant frustration and the corroding worries of the people who are before us Sunday after Sunday. We sit where they sit, wear their shoes, and if we are genuinely sympathetic, not merely walk into their hearts and minds but into their skins! We know what they fear and understand why they are so often defeated. (Gerald Ray Jordan, *You Can Preach: Building and Delivering the Sermon* [Westwood, N.J.: Revell, 1951], p. 218)

Life-situation preaching saves the preacher and his people from the fog of vague generalities. It delivers them from preaching that is largely merely spraying the universe with words. Some sermons could be likened to hover crafts skimming over the water on blasts of hot air. They never seem to land at any specific place. Profundity is not the crying need but rather simplicity coupled with directness. Sermons must build bridges to behavior.

The Definition of Life-situation Preaching

ADDRESSES NEED OF THE HEARERS

Life-situation preaching originates in the experience of the people and deals with a felt difficulty. When the preacher speaks to the suffering, he will never lack for a congregation. There is a burdened heart in every pew.

The average member of a congregation will not be satisfied by a debate about the author of the passage of Scripture or the minister's account of a conference he attended. The listener in the pew will not be satisfied by another fulmination on the preacher's pet peeve. The person in the pew is in need of concerned preaching. He longs for preaching by an individual who knows and loves his people. When we preach to people, we are not just giving them a lecture. We are intervening in their lives in the name of Jesus and through the ministry of the Holy Spirit to help, warn, console, and encourage.

Clarence S. Roddy says in regard to the life-situation sermon: "The sermon grows out of a life situation known to the pastor. He presents an existential problem which calls for a solution from the Word of God. . . . It must always be kept in mind that the solution is not found in the characters involved but in their God, in Christ."[1]

APPLIES MEANINGS OF RELEVANT SCRIPTURES

The preacher's reason for being in the pulpit is that he has the Word of the Lord to deliver to his hearers. The preacher must preach positively, telling the hearer what is true, setting God before his heart, and bidding him to come to Christ. Christian preaching must always be rooted in the purpose Jesus announced for His coming: "I came that they might have life, and might have it abundantly" (John 10:10).

JOINS TREND IN RECENT PREACHING

Life-situation preaching by name is a fairly recent kind of preaching. In one sense, preachers have always been concerned with the needs of men. The gospel is designed for such needs. Charles F. Kemp argues that the great interest in the 1940s and 1950s in this kind of preaching was caused by the pastoral psychology movement, which was due to the development of the psychological and sociological studies of man and resulted in a growing interest in counseling. Pioneer work in this field was done by such men as Richard Cabot, Russell Dicks, Anton Boisen, Seward Hiltner, and others. Preachers began to see the sermon as a tool with therapeutic value, if applied to the problems of the people in the pew.

A survey of sixty-eight homiletics textbooks, written by American-born teachers of homiletics between 1834 and 1954, indicated that the life-situation sermon per se was not referred to in those texts prior to 1944. It also pointed out that the four outstanding books dealing with this kind of preaching were: *In the Minister's Workshop*, by Halford Luccock; *The Preparation of Sermons*, by Andrew Blackwood; *You Can Preach*, by Gerald R. Jordan; and *Preaching Angles*, by Frank Caldwell.[2]

Luccock, in his book *In the Minister's Workshop*, says that the life-situation sermon originates in the experience of the people to whom it is preached, with the specific aim of bringing help to their life situation.

THE TERMINOLOGY OF LIFE-SITUATION PREACHING

This type of problem preaching has been referred to by different authors each using distinctive terminology:

It has been referred to as *life-situation* preaching by Luccock in *In the Minister's Workshop*, by Blackwood in *Preparation of Sermons*, by Jordan in *You Can Preach*, by Caldwell in *Preaching Angles*, and by Charles Kemp in *Life-Situation Preaching*.

Caldwell referred to it as *problem-solving* preaching as well.

James Cleland in *Preaching to be Understood* calls it *bifocal* preaching.

George Gibson in *Planned Preaching* refers to it as *personal problem* preaching.

David MacLennan and Henry Sloan Coffin called it *pastoral* preaching.

Edmond Linn in *Preaching as Counseling* which is a summary of Harry Emerson Fosdick's homiletical method, refers to this type of preaching as *counseling* preaching.

Wayne Oates in *The Christian Pastor,* calls it *therapeutic* preaching.

Charles Jefferson, in his two books, *The Minister as a Prophet* and *The Minister as a Shepherd,* refers to it as *preventive* preaching.

The term *ethical* preaching is given to it by James Hoppin in *The Office and Work of the Christian Ministry.*

Robert J. McCracken published *The Making of the Sermon.* In that book he referred to it as *social* preaching.

THE NEED FOR LIFE-SITUATION PREACHING

IT IS COMMON

Good preaching can be an important factor in the revitalization of the twentieth-century church. People are crying out as they did in years past, "Is there a word from the Lord?" (Jer. 37:17).

Edgar Jackson says, "Jesus spent little time sawing sawdust. He ripped into the real problems of people and of His age. He generated participation and response."[3] God had one Son, who came to earth as a preacher and teacher. He was touched with the joys, hopes, and pains of the people. He mingled with them in the crowds and ministered to them as individuals. He brought a word to the people from God the Father designed to make the loads lighter and the days brighter.

Biblically oriented life-situation preaching will never go out of style for it is designed to help people resolve the tensions, relieve the pressures, and disperse despair. The preacher strives to reach into the core of distress in personal, modern living and apply the healing of the gospel.

IT IS PASTORAL

The goals of pastoral care and prophetic preaching are quite compatible. Pastoral preaching should develop as a man of God becomes involved in the lives of the members of the congregation. He will become saturated with their situation and will then prayerfully seek to relate the revelation of God to the experiences of the people.

Our people need help. We have said through the years that Jesus saves, keeps, and satisfies. Our people are now asking that we make good on our proclamation. We must feed the appetite we have created. Preaching must recognize people and their problems. The preacher stands between the demands of God and the needs of man. When faith and the issues of life come together, light comes. It is as though two great electrodes have met and the fire has ignited.

Homiletical orthodoxy should combine the good news of the gospel and the contemporary situation. We need more sermons that try to face the real problems of the people, help meet their difficulties, answer their questions, confirm their noblest faith, and interpret their experiences with sympathetic understanding and compassion. The prophetic responsibility that rests upon the preacher cannot be fulfilled until the preacher speaks to the needs of the people in the pews in a way that can be understood and acted upon by them.

The sermon offers a minister one of his most valuable opportunities to enhance the mental and spiritual health of his people. As in group counseling, effective preaching offers an efficient means of helping a number of individuals simultaneously. From a mental health viewpoint the sermon has both preventive and therapeutic potentialities. It offers the Christian minister a superb opportunity to communicate the Christian message in a supportive, life-affirming, and growth-stimulating way.

Preaching is proclaiming the good news of transforming love, but the proclamation can be heard only if it is directly related to the dilemmas, problems, and decisions that people face in their daily living. A church should become an island of sanity in our neurotic society, avoiding thing-centeredness and keeping people at its heart.

IT IS DIVERSIFIED

Let us say that a hypothetical minister serves a congregation of five hundred adults representing a cross section of the American population. Based on various research studies, it could be estimated that approximately twenty-five of his members have been hospitalized for major mental illness in the past, twenty-four are alcoholics, another fifty are severely handicapped by neurotic conflicts, and another one hundred afflicted by moderate neurotic symptoms.[4]

One hundred fifteen members of the hypothetical congregation would answer "yes" to the question, "Have you ever felt you were going to have a nervous breakdown?" Seventy would have sought professional help for a personal or marital problem in the past. [5]

Approximately six of the parishoners will be hospitalized for mental illness in any given year. One member of his congregation will attempt suicide every other year. Eight members will be involved in a serious crime in a given year.

IT IS CHALLENGING

There is a need for the preacher today to proclaim the good news of the gospel in such a way that men will be drawn to God, to announce it in such a way that they will see its beauty and power, and to preach it in such a way that they will be able to put its truth into daily practice. Robert McCracken commented, "The pulpit is under obligation to urge Christians as citizens to come to grips with these evils [corruption. graft, juvenile and adult delinquency, drunkenness, gambling, bad houses, and unfair labor practices] and subdue them."[6]

Leslie Tizard said, "Whoever will become a preacher must feel the needs of men until it becomes an oppression to his soul."[7] Jesse McNeil puts it this way: "The preacher-prophet today who concerns himself with the ethical and social relationships of organized community life as a spokesman for God stands in the best tradition of the true prophets of old and follows in the footsteps of his Lord and Master, Jesus Christ."[8]

The sermon dealing with a problem should aim to comfort men and women with the comfort whereby we are comforted by the Holy Spirit, thus imparting the comfort of God. It should show the joy of the Lord to troubled souls. In his biography, Harry Emerson Fosdick describes the focus of effective preaching: "Every sermon should have for its main business the head-on constructive meeting of some problem which was puzzling minds, burdening consciences, distracting lives, and no sermon which has met a real human difficulty, with light to throw on it and help to win a victory over it, could possibly be futile."[9]

Fosdick recalls the decisive turning point in his own preaching. After he had known for some time that counseling could achieve results, he experienced a transition. He writes, "It was a great day when I began to feel that a sermon could be immediately creative and transforming."[10]

THE DISCOVERY FOR LIFE-SITUATION PREACHING

There are several means whereby the preacher may discover problems on which he may preach.

THROUGH PASTORAL CONTACT

One of the best is through pastoral calling. Pastoral calling should never be viewed as an appendix to the ministry, but rather as a very vital corollary to it. It is through visiting that we learn the specific needs of our people. If a man is going to preach to personal needs, it is necessary that he know what those needs are. This means pastoral work. If a man merely reads books, he may become a scholar; but if he separates himself from people, he will never become a preacher.

Hospital visitation will also enlighten the pastor regarding problems on which the people need special guidance and help. He will encourage the patient to speak about things that matter most. He will try to assure the person of God's healing power, love, care, and presence.

As he carries on conversations with his parishioners after services, problems will present themselves. He will seek guidance from the Holy Spirit for dealing with these at a later time through counseling outside the pulpit or through preaching.

THROUGH THOUGHTFUL QUESTIONS

He will want to pay attention to questions raised by the young people within the church. These questions will often indicate areas of special need and concern. One national evangelist holding meetings at the Paladium in Hollywood, California, restricted the audience to those between fifteen and twenty-five years of age. Slips of paper and pencils were distributed, and the young people were asked to write a question they would like to have answered. These were used as bases for messages on the succeeding evenings of the campaign.

Times of emergency provide topics dealing with special needs.

Newspapers, weekly magazines, and digests will also give the sermonizer an indication of concerns that are foremost in the thinking of the people of his day.

THROUGH BIBLE STUDY

As the sermonizer studies his Bible, he should keep in mind some of the problems of his people. He will thereby seek to find some biblical help to share with his congregation as he deals with their problems.

Someone has said that every need known to man is described in the Bible. There's the jealousy of Saul, the loyalty of Jonathan, the courage of Nathan, the despair of Jeremiah, and the struggles of Paul. Jacob was beset with the malady of a guilty conscience. God had a cure for this in Genesis 32:22-32. There was Elijah and his problem of discouragement. God had a cure for him in 1 Kings 19:1-18. There was Job with his question regarding the meaning of suffering. God had an answer for him as He put him through the "School of Suffering," especially in Job 42. Isaiah was troubled by despondency, but God had an answer for him in Isaiah 6. Daniel faced the problem of maintaining godliness in the midst of ungodly surroundings. His secret whereby this problem could be met and overcome is recorded in Daniel 6.

Every emotion experienced by man is described in the Psalms; crippling emotions such as guilt, doubt, futility, and fear. Also found is the assurance of forgiveness, the belief in the value of the individual, the challenge to self-forgetting service, the message of the transforming power of love, and an unquestioning and unfaltering faith that makes life strong and gives it meaning.

THROUGH GENERAL AWARENESS

A knowledge of the common problems of all mankind supplies numerous possibilities for life-situation preaching. Some of these problem areas are:

Adultery	Doubt	Jealousy
Adversity	Envy	Loneliness
Affliction	Failure	Lying
Anger	Fear	Nervousness
Anxiety	Frustration	Poverty
Apathy	Futility	Prejudice
Backsliding	Gossip	Presumption
Complacency	Guilt feelings	Pride
Compromise	Handicaps	Procrastination
Covetousness	Hypocrisy	Profanity

Cowardice	Immorality	Resentment
Death	Impatience	Selfishness
Depression	Inconsistency	Sorrow
Despair	Indifference	Suffering
Despondence	Inferiority	Temper
Disappointment	Ingratitude	Temptation
Dishonesty	Insecurity	Tension
Disobedience	Intolerance	Unhappiness
Divorce	Irresponsibility	Worry

THE HISTORY OF LIFE-SITUATION PREACHING

A study of the history of preaching reveals that preaching on problems has been employed by preachers for many years. F. R. Webber in his work *A History of Preaching* indicates that the friars in pre-Reformation Scotland (sixteenth century) "were content to condemn the evils of their day: drunkenness, profanity, theft, immorality and cruelty."[11] Edwin Charles Dargan indicates that similar preaching was done also in the fifteenth century. The Moderates, a liberal party in the Scottish church of the late seventeenth and eighteenth centuries, employed what might be called life-situation preaching.

Webber later points out that as this tendency kept recurring in the church, the emphasis upon sin and salvation would often be diminished. In the third volume of his work, Webber states: "In many instances there is less doctrinal preaching, but rather is there an indication of stress upon the ethical and the practical. The American pulpit, which has always been influenced by Europe, is beginning to make a contribution of its own to the history of preaching, and an American style is in the process of development."[12]

Great issues in America made life-situation preachers out of many. The issues of slavery and prohibition were two such issues. Webber goes on to state that "in our day it has become the fashion to discuss personality problems in the pulpit."[13] Ronald Sleeth also takes note of the shift toward life-situation preaching.[14]

SOME EXAMPLES OF LIFE-SITUATION PREACHING

If we were to make a list of some of the preachers who have been noted for preaching upon problems, whether personal, community, or national, we might include such men as:

Albert W. Beaven (1882-1943), with his fireside sermons.
Henry Ward Beecher (1813-1887), with his sermons against drinking, gambling, and slavery.

Walter Russell Bowie (1882-1968), with his emphasis upon the problems faced by university students.

Horace Bushnell (1802-1876), with his emphasis upon pastoral work and counseling.

Jack Finegan (1908-), with his emphasis upon the problems faced by university students.

Harry Emerson Fosdick (1878-1969), with his emphasis upon the fact that every sermon should have as its main business the solving of some problem.

Robert McCracken (1904-1973), Harry Emerson Fosdick's successor at the Riverside Church in New York.

Norman Vincent Peale (1898-), with his emphasis upon the power of positive thinking as he seeks to meet the common man's problems.

F. W. Robertson (1816-1853), with his concern for the intellectual and social problems of his day, thus arousing suspicion on the part of his conservative Christian colleagues.

Leslie Weatherhead (1893-1976), with his emphasis upon the correlation between psychology and religion.

SOME METHODS FOR LIFE-SITUATION PREACHING

INITIAL ANALYSIS

The sermonizer now faces the task of constructing a sermon that will discuss problems in terms of daily living and scriptural revelation in order that he, the preacher, may share with his people a possible cure or solution. One homiletics writer has suggested a four-point method of studying a problem prior to preaching:

Where are we?
How did we get here?
Where do we want to go?
How do we get there?

Another writer has suggested the following three points.

The problem: this is the situation.
The principle: this is the basis on which it may be solved.
The program: this is the way to solve it.

SUGGESTED PROCEDURE

A discussion method has been developed for directing thought in the resolution of a problem. This discussion method involves an adaptation of Professor John Dewey's analysis. An outline of this discussion method can be found in the book by J. H. McBurney and K. G. Hance.[15] It includes five steps.

Step 1. The defining of the problem. Reflective thinking has its inception in some kind of felt difficulty, perplexing situation, or problem. Our task is first to locate the problem as definitely as possible.

Step 2. The analyzing of the problem. This is an attempt to find out what is wrong and what is causing the trouble. It is an attempt to discover the nature of the problem in terms of its causal relationships.

Step 3. The solving of the problem. By a solution we merely mean an hypothesis or a proposal offered tentatively as a possible cure or suggestion. Various options are set forth, and a preferred solution is singled out. This is where the preacher will turn to the Scriptures for a plan.

Step 4. The resolving of the problem. This shows the development of proposed solutions from the preceding step. It includes a weighing and comparing of the relative merits of alternate solutions. Each option is evaluated in terms of the causes of the problem and the most effective resolution of it. Here biblical procedures are implemented.

Step 5. The disposing of the problem. It is profitable for a group to review carefully the steps that they will need to take in putting the proposed solutions into operation. This step is final verification of the problem/solution scenario. Here biblical goals are set forth.

Some Dangers of Life-Situation Preaching

Several dangers seem to be especially associated with this type of preaching.

One of the prominent dangers is connected with the violation of confidence. The sermonizer must beware of this temptation.

As he deals with the problem from the pulpit, he must beware of handling it inadequately; for to deal with the problem in such a fashion may do far more damage than good.

He must remember that to merely talk about a problem does not solve the problem.

There is also the danger of substituting psychology for Christianity.

He must never come to the point where he feels that this kind of preaching will take the place of pastoral care. The two go hand in hand.

This type of preaching has an attraction for the preacher;

therefore, the sermonizer should beware lest he fall into the trap of preaching only this kind of sermon. Too much of this kind of preaching may force the people to give too little attention to God and His provisions for them.

Because of the abundance of materials available to the preacher from extrabiblical sources that deal with each type of problem, he should beware of the danger of allowing biblical content to be crowded out of the sermon.

An overemphasis on problem or life-situation preaching could make the preacher wholly occupied with the issues of time, rather than with issues of eternity. He would thereby become merely timely, but not timeless.

There is the danger of this kind of sermon resulting in being a mild editorial comment on a problem, with only a religious flavor to the content.

The sermonizer must beware of setting himself up as a psychoanalyst, rather than guiding those with needs severe to professional help.

There is the danger of starting a sermon on the discussion of a problem for which the sermonizer has no solution,

Too many problem-centered sermons may put problems into people's minds—problems not there previously. A listener may begin to imagine the symptoms of the problem under discussion.

There is always the danger of dealing with a problem not actually faced by the local congregation.

The danger also exists of providing instruction and illustration without personal application.

There is the danger of having such an emphasis upon problem preaching that he will exclude doctrinal preaching to the detriment of his congregation.

The danger entices of preaching an incomplete life-situation sermon by not bringing man to the cross for pardon and to the living Christ for life-giving power.

There is the danger of confusing Christian morality with natural virtue.

The final danger is that the preacher's message may be distorted by some emotional need of his own, demanding satisfaction. He should ask himself, "Am I preaching on the needs of my people or on my own needs?"

SOME MODELS FOR LIFE-SITUATION PREACHING

The following scriptural sermon starters demonstrate how biblical material can be helpful as the preacher seeks to deal with life situations in his preaching.

These short outlines show only titles, texts, and main points.

Title: God Has a Cure for an Inferiority Complex   Text: Exodus
3–4
   I. When you feel inadequate in your person, 3:11,
       God provides His presence, 3:12
  II. When you feel inadequate in prestige, 4:1,
       God provides His power, 4:2
 III. When you feel inadequate in your presentation, 4:10,
       God makes the necessary provisions, 4:11

Title: The Benefits of Confession   Text: Psalm 32
   I. Forgiveness, v. 5
  II. Protection, v. 7
 III. Direction, v. 8

Title: Dealing with Sin   Text: Psalm 51
   I. Praying in confession, v. 3
  II. Praying for God's cleansing, v. 2
 III. Praying for God's restoration, v. 12

Title: Feeling Insecure?   Text: Psalm 91
   I. Realize your position, v. 1
  II. Realize His provision, v. 15

Title: The Chill of Loneliness   Text: Psalm 102:1-28
   I. Remember that God is eternal, v. 12
  II. Remember that God is active, v. 13
 III. Remember that God can be contacted, v. 17

Title: God's Provision for Anxiety   Text: Matthew 6:25-34
   I. Recognize God's care, v. 26
  II. Recognize God's knowledge, v. 32
 III. Recognize God's promise, v. 33

Title: God Can Provide Indestructible Joy   Text: Philippians
1:3-26
   I. Joy comes through prayer, vv. 3-11
  II. Joy comes through having a sense of purpose, vv. 12-18
 III. Joy comes through having glorious prospects, vv. 19-26

This includes most of the formal elements of a sermon.

Subject: Discouragement   Text: 1 Kings 19:1-18
Theme: Overcoming discouragement
Title: *A Cure for Discouragement*
Introduction: "All discouragement is from the devil." Quote from
    Catherine Marshall
    Discouragement and our daily living
    Explanation:
    1. Show relationship between 1 Kings and discouragement
    2. Show the prevalence of discouragement within the Scrip-
      ture
Proposition: A Christian can overcome discouragement.
Transitional Sentence: A Christian can overcome discouragement
    by following the steps outlined in 1 Kings 19:1-18.

Main Points:
   I. *Make certain that you are prepared physically,* vv. 4-8
    "So he arose and ate and drank, and went in the strength of
    that food forty days and forty nights" v. 8.
    1. Subpoint
    Illustration
    2. Subpoint
    3. Application
  II. *Make certain that you are prepared spiritually,* vv. 9-14
    "And after the fire a sound of gentle blowing" v. 12*b*.
    "What are you doing here, Elijah?" v. 13*b*.
    1. Subpoint
    Illustration
    2. Subpoint
    3. Application
 III. *Make certain that you are involved in service,* vv. 15-18
    "And the Lord said to him, 'Go, return on your way to the wilder-
    ness of Damascus" v. 15.
    1. Subpoint
    Illustration
    2. Application
 IV. *Make certain that you are ready to work with others,* vv. 19-21
    "So he departed from there and found Elisha . . . and threw his
    mantle upon him" v. 19.
    Illustration
    1. Subpoint
    2. Subpoint
    3. Application
Conclusion: Therefore, we as Christians should take the neces-
    sary steps to overcome discouragement:
    1. Get ready physically
    2. Get ready spiritually
    3. Get involved in service
    4. Be ready to work with others

A SUMMARY OF LIFE-SITUATION PREACHING

One of the chief requirements for the sermonizer who is to preach on problems is what R. H. Edwards has called "person-mindedness." When he can sense the supreme significance of persons in our world, when he can get them into central focus, and when they count above everything else—only then can he be possessed with "person-mindedness." Only then can he have one of the first prerequisites for being an effective Christian preacher upon the problems of his people. The following poem points up this need in an interesting fashion.

> A parish priest of austerity,
> Climbed up in a high Church-steeple
> To be nearer God, that he might hand
> His word down to the people.
> And in sermon script he daily wrote
> What he thought was sent from heaven,
> And dropped it down on the people's heads
> Two times one day in seven!
> In his age, God said, "Come down and die,"
> And he cried out from his steeple,
> "Where art Thou, Lord?" and the Lord replied,
> "Down here among My people!"[16]

NOTES

1. Clarence S. Roddy, "The Classification of Sermons," in *Baker's Dictionary of Practical Theology,* ed. R. G. Turnbull (Grand Rapids: Baker, 1967), p. 58.

2. Lloyd M. Perry, "Trends and Emphases in the Philosophy, Materials and Methodology of American Homiletical Education as Established by a Study of Selected Trade and Textbooks Published Between 1834 and 1954" (Ph.D. diss., Northwestern University, 1961).

3. Edgar N. Jackson, *How to Preach to People's Needs* (New York: Abingdon, 1956), pp. 12-13.

4. W. L. Holt, Jr., "The Mental Disease Problem as Seen by the Practicing Physician." *Health Week,* November 1955, pp. 17-18.

5. Gerald Gurin, et al., *Americans View Their Mental Health* (New York: Basic Books, 1960), p. 304.

6. Robert J. McCracken, *The Making of the Sermon* (New York: Harper, 1956), p. 51.

7. Leslie J. Tizard, *Preaching: The Art of Communication* (New York: Oxford U., 1959), p. 22.

8. Jesse McNeil, *The Preacher-Prophet in Mass Society* (Grand Rapids: Eerdmans, 1961), p. 70.

9. Harry Emerson Fosdick, *Living of These Days: An Autobiography* (New York: Harper, 1956), p. 94.

10. Ibid., p. 99.

11. F. R. Webber, *A History of Preaching in Britain and America* (Milwaukee: Northwestern, 1955), 2:30.

12. Ibid., 3:136.

13. Ibid., 2:653-54.

14. Ronald E. Sleeth, *Proclaiming the Word* (Nashville: Abingdon, 1964), p. 86.

15. J. H. McBurney and K. G. Hance, *Discussion in Human Affairs* (New York: Harper, 1950), pp. 65-68.

16. Robert McCracken, *The Making of the Sermon* (New York: Harper, 1956), p. 37.

BIBLIOGRAPHY

Bryson, Harold T. and James C. Taylor. *Building Sermons to Meet People's Needs.* Nashville: Broadman, 1980.

Cleland, James T. *Preaching to be Understood.* Nashville: Abingdon, 1965.

Jefferson, Charles. *The Minister as a Prophet.* New York: Crowell, 1905.

_____.*The Minister as a Shepherd.* New York: Crowell, 1912.

* Kemp, Charles F. *Life Situation Preaching.* St. Louis: Bethany, 1958.

*_____ . *The Preaching Pastor.* St. Louis: Bethany, 1966.

Linn, Edmund H. *Preaching as Counseling.* Valley Forge: Judson, 1960.

MacLennan, David. *Pastoral Preaching.* Philadelphia: Westminster, 1955.

McCutcheon, James N. *The Pastoral Ministry.* Nashville: Abingdon, 1978.

* Oglesby, William B., Jr. *Biblical Themes for Pastoral Care.* Nashville: Abingdon, 1980.

* Perry, Lloyd M. and Charles M. Sell. *Speaking to Life's Problems.* Chicago: Moody, 1983.

Quayle, William A. *The Pastor-Preacher.* Grand Rapids: Baker, 1979.

Sangster, W. E. *The Approach to Preaching.* Philadelphia: Westminster, 1952.

* Stratman, Gary D. *Pastoral Preaching: Timeless Truth for Changing Needs.* Nashville: Abingdon, 1983.

Teikmanis, Arthur L. *Preaching and Pastoral Care.* Englewood Cliffs, N. J.: Prentice-Hall, 1964.

7

BIBLICAL PREACHING AND DOCTRINAL COMMUNICATION

> We are paying bitterly now, and we shall pay more bitterly yet, in the bewilderment of our youth, for the neglect by the church to educate its ministry in its own subject of plastic time. . . . When preachers denounce theology, or a Church despises it for literary or social charm, that is to sell the cross to be a pendant at the neck of the handsome world. It is spiritual poverty and boldness, it is not the simplicity in Christ, to be sick of grace, judgment, atonement and redemption. The holiness of God has become a spent force if a Gospel which turns entirely upon it is called metaphysical or academic. (Peter Forsyth, *The Cruciality of the Cross* [Grand Rapids: Eerdmans, 1909], pp. 49-50)

THE NEEDS FOR DOCTRINAL PREACHING

DILUTED CHRISTIANITY

The most serious menace to the church's mission is not secularism without, but diluted Christianity within; the religious generalities and innocuous platitudes of a pallid, anemic Christianity which is regarded simply as "the lowest common denominator" of many religions. William Barclay said:

> It is one of the disasters of modern times that the teaching ministry of the church has not been exercised as it should. There is any amount of topical preaching; there is any amount of exhortation; but there is little use in exhorting a man to be a Christian if he does not know what being a Christian means. Instruction is a primary duty of the Christian preacher.[1]

DEMONIC ZEAL

In a day when demonic forces of passionate evil have been unleashed upon the earth and fierce emotions are tearing the world apart, a milk-and-water passionless theology is worse than useless. A tepid Christianity is no match for a scorching paganism. The thrust of the demonic must be met with the fire of the divine. John Henry Jowett said:

> We must grapple with the big things, the things about which our people will hear nowhere else; the deep, the abiding, the things that permanently matter. We are not appointed merely to give good advice but to proclaim good news. Therefore must the apostolic themes be our themes: The holiness of God; the love of God; the grace of the Lord Jesus; the solemn wonders of the cross; the ministry of the divine forgiveness; the fellowship of His sufferings; the power of the Resurrection; the blessedness of divine communion; the heavenly places in Christ Jesus; the mystical indwelling of the Holy Ghost; the abolition of the deadliness of death; the ageless life; our Father's house; the liberty of the glory of the children.[2]

SPIRITUAL WEAKNESS

Doctrinal preaching tends to flourish or languish according to the ebb and flow of spiritual life in the church. When prophets and apostles, Luther and Calvin, preached doctrine, the church made an impact on the age. In what Kenneth S. Latourette labels "The Great Century," the nineteenth, the foremost pulpit masters relied largely on doctrine. Such preaching declined during the first half of the twentieth century. So did the influence of the church and the clergy.

PULPIT POWER

The decline in doctrinal preaching is not wholly attributable to a decline of interest in doctrine. It has occurred in part because of the difficulty preachers have in handling doctrine within the context of a sermon. This serious deficiency must be corrected in order to reproduce some of the past high points of pulpit impact.

Charles H. Spurgeon represented the best of the British pulpit a century ago. One of his early volumes, typical of many, contains twenty-seven sermons, more than half of them doctrinal.

Canon H. P. Liddon of St. Paul's Cathedral authored one volume that includes forty-two discourses, at least half of them doctrinal. Six concern the hereafter, including his famous discourse, "The First Five Minutes After Death" (1 Cor. 13:12).

On the American side of the Atlantic, doctrine abounds in the printed sermons of Horace Bushnell, Phillips Brooks, Henry Ward

Beecher, and many others of yesterday. In 1908, Grenville Kleiser's *The World's Great Sermons*, a well-known collection drawn largely from the sermons of nineteenth-century preachers, was published in ten small volumes. Of the 113 selections, more than half may be classified as doctrinal.

About the turn of the century men who issued books of sermons began to include fewer doctrinal messages. As early as 1905, Charles E. Jefferson, a gifted evangelical liberal, warned his brethren against the neglect of doctrine in the pulpit.

[A man] can give his sermon the Christian atmosphere and let a stream of Christian sentiment trickle through its paragraphs . . . without even so much as once referring to those fundamental dogmas by which the church of God lifted the Roman Empire off its hinges, and turned the stream of the centuries into a new channel. . . . Applied Christianity has been our theme; but alas, we have had too little Christianity to apply. . . . Moreover, the new preaching of Christianity with Christian dogma eliminated does not seem to be working well.[3]

EVANGELICAL OUTREACH

The central theme of Christian doctrinal preaching is human redemption in all its widespread ramifications and relations, accomplished through the incarnation, life, atoning death, and resurrection of Jesus Christ, the Son of God.

T. R. Glover was going home one night with a friend when he stopped suddenly and said emphatically, "I don't give tuppence for the man who goes into the pulpit to tell me what my duty is; but I give all I have to the man who tells me from whence my help cometh." As Dietrich Bonhoeffer suggested from his prison cell, we need to quit thinking of God as inhabiting the edges of life and think of Him as the center.

Professor John A. Broadus knew what he was talking about when he said that the Reformation was, before anything else, a reformation of preaching. The same will be true of any kind of reformation in our churches today that is significant and enduring.

To be truly edifying every sermon must have in it a doctrinal element. Let a sermon be ever so rich in exhortation, rebuke, and comfort; if it is devoid of doctrine, it is a lean and empty sermon, whose exhortation, rebuke, and comfort float in the air.

THE NATURE OF DOCTRINAL PREACHING

The doctrinal sermon is the culmination and crown of all sermonizing. It has been of supreme importance to most great preachers of the Christian church beginning with the apostle Paul himself.

The meaning of the term *doctrinal sermon* is fairly broad. The nature of doctrinal preaching is discovered in the practical, systematic exposition and application of biblical teaching from a living man to living people. This definition has eight elements that should be explained.

IT IS PRACTICAL

It makes doctrine relevant and vital to life. In short, doctrinal preaching is popular religious instruction from the pulpit. The doctrinal sermon calls for a practical explanation of important Christian truths in order to answer the unspoken questions of the hearers. The man in the pulpit must know the heart hunger of his people. The purpose of the message is to make the truth meaningful to the individual lives in the congregation.

IT IS SYSTEMATIC

When a particular doctrine is being expounded, it is handled with full awareness of the whole teaching of Scripture on that and related topics. All the biblical data is organized into a logical outline that results in a comprehensive doctrinal system. This assures that no detail of truth is either overlooked or overemphasized.

IT IS EXPOSITORY

It states, explains, interprets, and relates the texts that embody the Bible doctrine. The doctrinal sermon not only begins with the reading of biblical text(s) but it also progresses in a thorough and orderly unfolding of the meaning of that Scripture. Doctrinal preaching must be exegetical (deriving the meaning from the text) not eisegetical (attributing meaning to the text).

IT IS APPLICATIONAL

It shows the same relevance and timeliness of biblical truth to the people in the pews today as the divine and human authors of the Scriptures intended for the first recipients of the Word.

IT IS BIBLICAL

The Word is the source and foundation of the believer's commitment and faith, which are enlarged through preaching. Doctrinal preaching is the statement, exposition, interpretation, and application of biblical truth. The application brings timelessness and timeliness together. Relevance, concreteness, vividness, lucidity, progression, clarity, application, purposefulness, personalness, and persuasiveness are all characteristics of good doctrinal preaching. There must be faithfulness to the Bible in devotion and depth of study.

Faris Whitesell stated that "certain great, basic doctrines dominate the Scripture. Every Scripture passage is either directly or indirectly related to the doctrines of the Bible."[4] He also wrote:

> Doctrinal sermons generally are topical sermons. Usually a single Scripture text does not give the whole truth about a Bible doctrine. The doctrine must become the topic, and the whole range of Scripture passages bearing on that doctrine are used to yield up their contributions to that doctrine. In Biblical preaching, doctrinal sermons will go beyond books of theology and deal directly with what the Scriptures themselves have to say. . . . The topic controls the contents and developments of the sermon.[5]

IT IS TRUTH-CENTERED

It is the preacher's interpretation of a vital Christian truth for a practical purpose. The reference is to teachings found in the Scriptures, supremely in Christ and the cross. It is the logical statement of facts drawn from the texts bearing upon a certain teaching.

The doctrinal sermon must treat in particular the great fundamental truths of Holy Scripture, such as sin, grace, redemption, repentance, faith, conversion and regeneration, justification, adoption, sanctification, good works, providence, the means of grace, assurance of salvation, death, resurrection, judgment, everlasting life, and everlasting condemnation. The doctrinal sermon aims at clarifying and deepening the knowledge of salvation.

One of the besetting sins of modern preachers is to be content with little themes, instead of remembering that we are called to proclaim the good news of eternity. A preacher must teach what fellowship with God is, what believers find in their relation with Him, how communion with Him is established and maintained. That is doctrinal preaching, and it should form a large part of a minister's pulpit teaching each year.

IT IS PERSONAL

The message flows out from the continuous, consistent Bible study and spiritual experience in the life of the preacher. For this reason doctrinal preaching will bear the imprint of the personality and perspective of the preacher. While there is some danger in this, such a phenomena is consistent with the truth that spiritual gifts among the Body of Christ include human individuals (such as pastor-teachers) who are enabled to make unique contributions for the health of the church.

IT IS CONGREGATIONAL

One of the major challenges in doctrinal preaching is the use of words lay people can understand. John Wesley felt called of God to preach to illiterate multitudes. Before he spoke to his congregation he read his sermon manuscript to a domestic servant. He urged her to stop him at every word she did not understand. The manuscript was filled with lines and erasures. Wesley kept on, however, until he mastered a speaking style so plain and unpretentious that people in his congregation with no formal education whatsoever had little difficulty following his thought. In a volume of his sermons dated 1746, he said:

> I design plain truth for plain people. Therefore, of set purpose I abstain from all nice and philosophical speculations; from all perplexed and intricate reasonings; and, as far as possible, from even the show of learning. I labour to avoid all words which are not easy to be understood, and all which are not used in common life; and, in particular, those kinds of technical terms that so frequently occur in Bodies of Divinity; those modes of speaking which men of reading are intricately acquainted with, but which to common people are an unknown tongue.[6]

The Advantages of Doctrinal Preaching

David Yohn outlines three values of doctrinal preaching: it returns us to traditional doctrines of the church; it calls the people to conform to the church and the church not to conform to the world; and it takes, exegetes, explains, and applies one abiding doctrine.[7]

IT EXALTS THE WORD

Doctrinal preaching certainly gives honor to the gospel. It instructs and edifies the listener. It develops confidence in the reasonableness of Christianity. It adds to the intellectual character of the ministry. It clears up difficulties and misunderstandings that have gathered in the minds of the listeners with respect to important truths and facts of Christianity. Such preaching helps the listener discriminate between that which is primary and that which is secondary in Christian truth. It provides a firm foundation for effective ethical teaching and preaching.

IT EVANGELIZES THE LOST

Andrew Blackwood in his book *Doctrinal Preaching for Today* stated that in the past every evangelistic movement blessed of God has come largely through doctrinal preaching.

Two factors contributed supremely to the Evangelical Revival of the nineteenth century—John Wesley's preaching and Charles Wesley's hymns. Both these were firmly based on Christian doctrine. Far from being dull, abstract or academic, whether mediated through sermons or hymns, Christian doctrine is the very foundation and source of all true evangelism.[8]

IT REVIVES THE CHURCH

Many years ago Charles G. Finney said that there has never been a revival that was not brought about by doctrine, set forth with power and clearness. Phillips Brooks understood this same truth in 1877:

No preaching ever had any strong power that was not the preaching of doctrine. The preachers that have moved and helped men have always preached doctrine. No exhortation to a good life that does not put behind it some truth as deep as eternity can seize, can hold the conscience. Preach doctrine, preach all the doctrine that you know, and learn forever more and more; but preach it always not that men may believe it, but that men may be saved by believing it. So it shall be live not dead. So men shall rejoice in it and not decry it. So shall they feed on it at your hands as on the bread of life, solid and sweet, and claiming for itself the appetite which God made for it.[9]

Doctrinal preaching is not easy preaching, but its omission makes one a trifler. The very craft of preaching is to make theological facts shine with immense significance and become glowing truths by which people live. The real questions every thinking person wants answered amid the changes of this life are very few. Is God there? Does God care? Is there meaning in life? Does life continue after death? What is God's purpose with me? How can I get to heaven?

THE SPIRIT IN DOCTRINAL PREACHING

The ministry of the Holy Spirit in preaching is indispensable. The preacher must be well prepared spiritually, physically, intellectually, and emotionally—but it is the Holy Spirit alone who can bring about the combination of truth, clarity, and passion so as to make a sermon bring forth life.

The Holy Spirit, not the preacher, is responsible for conviction of sin, for illumination of the Word, for regeneration of the lost to new life in Christ, for sanctification to transform the believer into greater Christlikeness. Modern preaching, of whatever kind, needs the stirring, purifying, invigorating, and refreshing winds of the Holy Spirit.

On the part of the preacher there must be prevailing prayer, surrender, obedience, consecration, trust, and thorough preparation. Nevertheless, the most vital concern to effective, high quality doctrinal preaching is the ministry of the Holy Spirit in and through the servant of God.

THE CONTENT OF DOCTRINAL PREACHING

APPLIED EXPOSITION

The material of the doctrinal sermon is doctrine. Its object is to convince, and its method is proof. The emphasis within the doctrinal sermon will be more upon truth than upon duty. This does not mean, however, that a doctrinal sermon is merely a theological treatise. It is not the exposition of one or more doctrines irrespective of how important the doctrine may be. The doctrinal sermon is first of all a sermon; second, it is a *doctrinal* sermon. As a sermon it combines exposition with application.

The truth preached must be shown to be of supreme importance for Christian faith and life. James Russell Lowell said, "We need the tongue of the people in the mouth of the scholar." We must strive to reveal the relationship of the doctrine to Christian life and experience. The preacher must therefore be on the alert for ways of presenting old truths in new ways. In dealing with doctrine the preacher should be logical, progressive, and conclusive.

In his *Homiletics,* J. M. Reu lists three ways of making doctrinal sermons dry: by entering into subtle distinctions of dogmatics and forgetting the difference between the technical language of the specialist in theology and the saving knowledge of the Christian congregation; by failing to bring the truth of a doctrine to bear on practical daily living; and by forgetting to convey truth to the hearers with whom the preacher should have established personal, living contact.[10] There is no sure way to prevent the minds of the listeners from wandering, but if we translate the gospel into understandable, practical language, our cause will be advanced.

Merrill R. Abbey in his book *Living Doctrine in a Vital Pulpit* suggests that when preaching on doctrine we should make a double analysis both of the text and the congregation. The preacher should not only study his passage, but he should also study his people. He should be certain that doctrinal preaching will meet human needs. Two inferences may be drawn from this statement. One is that some doctrines are better taught in class than preached from the pulpit. A lesson consists of exposition, but a sermon combines exposition with application. Doctrines may be important but may not have direct bearing upon daily living.

The second inference is that doctrinal preaching must stress application. Spurgeon said that the sermon begins where the application begins. The good doctrinal preacher should be proficient in applying doctrinal truth to daily living. Dwight Stevenson in his work *In the Biblical Preacher's Workshop* states that the preacher must make the past tense of the text the present text of the listeners. Failure to stress the practical implications of doctrine is one of the major causes of people's dislike of doctrinal preaching.

THEOLOGICAL BREADTH

Gerald Judd states that the modern preacher needs to become an expert in biblical theology. He will find it helpful to group the doctrines of the Bible into two categories: "major doctrines" and "minor doctrines."[11] As he begins to study a Bible doctrine, he should collect the references to that doctrine. He can do this by tracing a doctrinal word directly in the Scriptures or with the aid of an analytical concordance or topical Bible. A survey of some books on Bible doctrine will also help him at this point. The following books provide an introductory survey of some of the major doctrines:

> *The Great Doctrines of the Bible,* William Evans
> *In Understanding Be Men,* T. C Hammond
> *Know What You Believe,* Paul E. Little

As he locates the Scripture references, the preacher should define the doctrine by comparing all the references and by using such extrabiblical helps as may be necessary. The doctrinal references should be related to their scriptural context and also to the total pattern of biblical truth. The doctrine should then be related to personal experience. What difference does this truth make in daily living?

CONTEMPORARY RELEVANCE

Expository doctrinal preaching is not without its dangers. One is that of seeming to deal with the past rather than the present action of God in the Word. It is better to begin with something contemporary and then relate that to the content of the biblical passage on which one is preaching. In preparing a sermon, present what the passage stresses. In almost every preaching section of Holy Scripture, either a doctrine or a duty predominates.

The task of translating doctrinal truth into the realm of practical living consists of two steps. The preacher must regularly study the biblical truths until he understands what they meant to the people for whom they were first written. Then he must make the transition from ancient to modern times, showing what the same truths should mean to his congregation. The message of the Bible must be clothed in the thought forms of the modern world. The truth should be applied as the preacher goes along, from the first paragraph to the last. What difference does Christian faith make in people's decisions? In their ordeals? In their obligations? In their manners? In their resources? In their appreciation? In their hopes? Many sermons are intelligent but irrelevant.

Language is deeper than words, however; it is concerned with meanings. That is why the cry to change the vocabulary of Christianity to twentieth-century language remains largely a plaintive one. Although jargon is to be avoided, there is a great deal of difference between using specialized words and using traditional religious language in a meaningful way. Many who desire to change religious terminology really wish to get rid of the concepts behind the words.

The key to relevance in doctrinal preaching lies in the ability of the preacher to make his material real to those who sit in front of him. This is the acid test of preaching doctrinally.

Dietrich Ritschl in *A Theology of Proclamation* suggests that pastors ought to hold planning sessions with laity, allowing them opportunity to help choose the sermon texts, and together they reach some general agreement on the interpretation and application of the texts chosen.

BIBLICAL SUBSTANCE

If the first word about preaching doctrine concerns relevance, with concern for language, meaning, and analogy, the second major word to be said about doctrinal preaching is that it should be biblical. We have defined biblical preaching as the proclamation of the good news of the gospel through specific biblical materials in a relevant way. There is no place in the Christian pulpit for preaching that is not genuinely and thoroughly biblical.

The preacher must not take anything for granted as he presents the message. He must patiently define his terms, illustrate his concepts, and use simple analogies from daily life to clarify his ideas. He must be careful not to give too much material too fast. The listeners must have time to digest the subject matter. It is important to summarize the doctrinal material several times during the message.

SERMONIC VARIETY

The content of doctrinal preaching might take the form of any one of several sermonic forms.

Direct doctrinal presentation. The types of sermons we discuss here all present doctrine directly. In some ways direct doctrinal preaching parallels the development one finds in a systematic theology book but with the addition of application.

1. The apologetical sermon. One type of doctrinal sermon is based upon apologetics. It presents a reasoned defense of Christianity against the attacks of its critics by marshaling evidences for Christianity. This sermon deals with the relationship of the Christian faith to the wider sphere of a man's secular knowledge. Its aim is to show that faith is not at variance with the Truth.

The style of such a sermon is didactic, sound in logic, and intellectually challenging. The preacher should avoid using technical language. Is it wise to use in the pulpit a technical term such as *incarnation*? The word does not appear in the Bible and does not interest most laymen. As a rule a pastor-preacher should not talk in technical terms that, to laymen, seem abstract and impersonal. In a doctrinal sermon, however, one such word may have to appear, and that quite often. Either the pulpit should fill such a term as *incarnation* with old light and new meaning, or else the church ought to discard its historical vocabulary. To discard it now would look strangely like forsaking the Christianity of the New Testament. So let us translate every such word into thought-forms of our day, but limit ourselves to only one technical term in each doctrinal sermon.

In combating false systems of belief it is important to show that these systems are opposed to Christianity and not just to the opinions of the preacher. False systems should be studied very carefully and thoroughly before attempting to show their conflict with Christianity. The preacher should remember that the presumption of truth is on the side of Christianity and that the burden of proof rests with contrary positions.

2. The polemical sermon. Another type of doctrinal sermon is based upon polemics. Such a sermon deals with the many varieties of opinion, differences, and theories within the Christian church. Much of the controversy of the first half of the twentieth century was polemical, not apologetical.

When this type of doctrinal sermon is presented, it is not wise to deride or ridicule any group. Attacks should not be made on positions where the Bible is not clearly explicit. The preacher should never appear arrogant, condescending, or hypercritical in his attitude.

It is important for the preacher to discover the true meaning of the passages quoted based upon the original text of Scripture. He should relate the whole biblical pattern of thought to the problem being discussed. Such an approach will assist the preacher in being consistent and thorough.

3. The declarative sermon. Another type of doctrinal sermon

is the declarative sermon. This type of message sets forth a doctrine without attempting to defend the doctrine against attacks from within or from without the church. The declarative sermon is similar to the sermon of affirmation referred to by Gerald Ray Jordon in *You Can Preach* (1951). The main characteristic of this type of sermon is the bringing up to date of the truth once presented by our forefathers in dogmatic fashion. Sermons on the creeds are readily adaptable to this pattern.

Indirect doctrinal presentation. Doctrine can also be presented indirectly. Whereas doctrine is usually presented directly by apologetic, polemic, or declarative sermons, doctrine is usually presented indirectly by means of the biographical sermon.

1. Definition of the doctrinal-biographical sermon. This type of sermon is developed by showing how a doctrine is demonstrated in the life and experience of a Bible character who serves as an example to the listener. The listener will be apt to apply the truth to himself because "the Bible is a hall of mirrors and wherever men look within its pages they see themselves reflected."[12]

2. Examples of the doctrinal-biographical sermon. Think about the providence of God in the life of a busy man. Instead of arguing about the matter of trying to prove it by logic, one may point out evidence for it in the life of Joseph. Instead of preaching about sin and pardon as pale, grey abstractions, the preacher may turn to King David as a living object lesson. After a sermon about the God of Isaac, a lay officer said to the pastor, "I wish you would preach about the God of Jacob; most of us laymen are more like him than we are like his father." The resulting sermon about Jacob dealt with the best thing we know about God, His inexhaustible mercy, and was titled "The God of a Wicked Man."

3. Practitioners of the doctrinal-biographical sermon. Men of yesterday, such as Frederick W. Robertson, Dwight L. Moody, Alexander Maclaren, Clarence E. Macartney, and A. B. Simpson were all known for their proclamation of doctrine through Bible characters. In Unitarian Boston, for twenty-four years (1869-93), Phillips Brooks preached doctrine indirectly. Of his 200 sermons published in a ten-volume collection, at least half are of this kind. More recently, James S. Stewart of Edinburgh also sometimes employs the indirect approach to doctrinal preaching.

4. Advantages of the doctrinal-biographical sermon.

Doctrine and ethics can be preached in connection with life.
A difficult doctrine can be presented more easily.
The Bible character furnishes the best illustration of the doctrine's application.
Truth can be presented in a palatable manner.

Truth can be understood more readily.
Current dislike for doctrine can be overcome.
A new area of Bible study will be opened to the people.
The appeal is to reason.
It provides an indirect approach to subjects best not approached directly.

5. Dangers of the doctrinal-biographical sermon.

Do not emphasize the person more than the doctrine.
Do not rely upon memory.
Do not generalize the life or doctrine.
Do not attempt to include all the details.
Use scriptural undergirding; do not fail to keep to this rule.
Do not omit application.
Do not obscure the doctrine or life with overemphasis of either.
Do not employ technical language often.
Do not limit yourself to pleasing, or familiar, people and doctrines.
Do not exaggerate in order to impress.

THE APPLICATIONS IN DOCTRINAL PREACHING

NEED OF DOCTRINAL APPLICATIONS

Ezekiel Robinson stated that "no doctrine can be fully understood by us, much less effectively preached, until we have worked ourselves out into a clear apprehension of its meaning and power through Christian experience."[13] What the truth has done at the heart of the preacher is what the truth will do at the heart of his people. Fresh, personal encounter with the Word will produce fresh application to the heart.

Timely application will bring the message of the Bible to bear upon life at a point of need. This requires a personal understanding of the doctrine from experience, an understanding of people, a clear, accurate statement of the doctrine through focus upon the text, and a carefully phrased and worded application. James Black instructs the preacher to "choose words like delicate porcelain."[14]

Timeless truth can answer the question people are asking; it can have bite, edge, muscle, and drive. The ancient revelation can be important and vital to our present needs. "Every sermon should have as its main business the head-on constructive meeting of some problem which puzzles the mind, burdens the conscience, distracts the life, rejoices the heart, undergirds the faith of the people."[15]

All doctrinal preaching can be practical if the message is aimed at the heart and if the messenger is close enough to his people to know where they need help, instruction, and strengthening.

With timeless truth in one hand and timely application in the other, the duty of the preacher is to bring them together in the spoken word. Application sets doctrine into living principles of life.

Timely application of timeless truth will result in a balance between doctrine and duty. "Analyze a doctrine and you will find it to be only the theoretic statement of duty; analyze a duty, and you will find it to be the perceptive form of a doctrine."[16] Just as a tree grows from a root system, so a duty grows from doctrine.

Timely applications carry the quality of a knock on the door. They set forth a certain course of action attractively. They are a plea, a stimulus, a call, or an invitation to do something. They will appeal to the hearers in one of three ways:

Security appeals offer a sense of confidence and belonging (life, salvation, service).

Acquisitive appeals induce the hearer to personal achievements (peace, power).

Social and ethical appeals seek correct conduct in the hearer (equality, fellowship, duty).

Application means to relate, to involve, to move to action. Application means to show to the audience that they can use and put to a practical personal use the truth of the message. Application shows the hearer how he can solve problems, live a better life, please God, and perform other spiritual acts and duties. It is the natural companion for explanation. As explanation presents the message of God's "then," so application presents the message of God's "now."[17]

In application there is the relevance of the truth, the clarity of the truth, and the answer of the truth to the question, "So what?" In an effort to apply doctrine, R. C. H. Lenski stated that there is a negative and a positive channel of application: as then—so now (what was true to those people is equally true for us now), and as then—so not now.[18]

Charles Spurgeon reminded the preacher of the Word that some people "are dead, you must rouse them; some are troubled, you must comfort them; others are burdened, you must point them to the Burden-bearer. Still more are puzzled, you must enlighten and guide them; still others are careless and indifferent, you must warn and woo them."[19]

FUNCTIONS OF DOCTRINAL APPLICATIONS

Make truth relevant. Application shows appropriateness, fitness, suitability of the message to men. It shows practical, usable, personal means whereby the hearer can solve problems, live a better life, please God, or fulfill spiritual duties.

The doctrinal message combines what a man is to believe concerning God and what a man is to do for God through the process of application. The hearer is directed to believe some doctrine and then encouraged to behave in a manner consistent with it. Duty is based upon belief.

The focus of application seeks to make the biblical doctrine clear, interesting, significant, vivid, convincing, and effective to the hearers.

It should be noted that a factor that will control the amount of time spent in developing application within the sermon is the complexity of the truth being presented. A presentation of a doctrine that seems complex or remote to the audience will demand more carefully planned and more time-consuming applications than simpler ones. On the other hand, the less elaborate the doctrinal sermon, the less cultivated the audience, or the more emotional the hearers, the more rapidly the application can be made.

The speaker ought to be immersed in life; not that his sermons may never escape from the local details, but rather since, being in contact with life nearest him, he may state his gospel in terms of human experience. For a message to be enriching, two realities must be married: the truth of God and the need of man.

Applications will be involved in joining together some amazing opposites.

Time and eternity	Doctrine and duty
Creed and conduct	Head and heart
Fuel and fire	Past and present
Scholarship and simplicity	Reverence for God and
Ancient Scripture and	respect for individuals
contemporary life	

Teach practical procedures. Application should be present in a message because many of those in the audience lack the special spiritual, hermeneutical, and mental skills necessary to apply the truth of the sermon to themselves. Moreover, many lack the will and desire to apply spiritual truth to sensitive areas of their lives.

W. E. Sangster proposes that any speaker should hang up the word "how" over his desk to remind himself that message preparation is not complete until the task of application is done.

Application facilitates change. It not only clarifies the responsibility the individual must ascertain in the truth of the sermon but also how that responsibility is to be fulfilled or carried out. The focus is upon the individual: a definite person with a definite need finding definite application of a definite doctrine or truth. Apply the Word to real people who have names, faces, ages, addresses, needs, and potential.

The application must be personal, but it must also include means and methods. How to do it must always follow the exhortation to do it. This may well be the weakest point in most presentations. The application, then, should deal with particulars.

The application process is important because it clarifies the responsibility of individuals to the truth being proclaimed. It also clarifies how the person is to fulfill that responsibility. Application is a moral or spiritual term denoting the use to be made of the sermon.

Establish priority needs. If a doctor, arriving at the scene of an accident, knows that he has only twenty minutes at most in which to save a victim's life, he will waste none of them combing the patient's hair or brushing his clothes or checking marks of identification. He will move as swiftly as he can to the most critical and threatening wound and will address to it all his skills and supplies. He deals immediately with the most serious threat to life. The speaker has his twenty minutes, more or less, in which to bring life to someone within his hearing or in which to let him die. There is no time for the tea and cookies of amiable conversation.

Demand moral action. Application may be called the personal side of the sermon. The oasis of the speaker's handling of doctrine on the level of relevance finally comes down to how real he can make his material to those who sit in front of him.

David Randolph uses the word "concretion" to refer to the "process whereby the meaning of the biblical text is brought to expression in the situation of the hearers." The message is carried forth into life. Application plants the word in the affections and secures revival of heart and uplifting of life.

A. W. Tozer puts it this way:

> There is scarcely anything so dull and meaningless as Bible doctrine taught for its own sake. Truth divorced from life is not truth in the biblical sense, but something else and something less. . . . No man is better for knowing that God in the beginning created the heaven and the earth. The devils knows that, and so did Ahab and Judas Iscariot. No man is better for knowing God so loved the world of men that He gave His only begotten Son for their redemption. In hell there are millions who know that. Theological truth is useless until it is obeyed. The purpose behind all doctrine is to secure moral action.[20]

James T. Cleland uses the term "bifocal preaching" in explaining the importance of applying biblical truth to contemporary listeners. He states that "bifocal preaching is doctrinal preaching, because all sound preaching is doctrinal. The preacher is the doctor of a doctrine."[21]

Avoid barren orthodoxy. Doctrinal preaching is not concerned with facts and references in isolation but in relationship to life. Facts are the framework and dynamic of doctrinal preaching, but without timely application they will become stagnant. Doctrinal preaching and teaching must not only relate the truth; it must apply the truth and put it to the test immediately.

Without application, the message is a fishing line without a hook. A sure way to make biblical doctrine dull and meaningless is to forget application. "Theological truth is useless until it is obeyed."[22] A message without application is like a lecture on general health without a written prescription. A message is as useless as a lost nail if it is not directed and driven home.[23]

Faris Whitesell includes eleven pages on power through application in his book. Application that is sound and forceful results from lifting the truth from its local and temporary context in the Bible so that it meets a timeless and universal need. A message without application is a monologue.[24]

A double bridge must be built and crossed by the speaker before he can use application with effect. He must move his audience from the biblical world to the modern world. He must also move his audience from the act of listening to a speaker to an act of personal participation with the speaker as he witnesses to God's self-discourse in Christ.[25] Doctrine alone helps a person to interpret the experiences of life, but the application of doctrine illuminates the experience of life. "The end of Christian doctrine is to teach men how to live a good and holy life."[26]

James Stalker points out that Paul unites doctrine with duty in all his letters, that he always takes the step from creed to conduct. "In Paul's mind all the great doctrines of the Gospel were living fountains of motives for well doing: and even the smallest and commonest duties of everyday life were magnified and made sacred by being connected with the facts of salvation."[27]

Overcome negative attitudes. Within any congregation one will find three fundamental elements of resistance. The first is physical: "We are really tired. We are all indifferent. We are all inert. You cannot interest us." The second is personal: "The man has a good line. He's interesting some. But there's nothing in it for me." The third is pugilistic: "Come, come now. I've been very patient with you. I defy you to prove your case." In a Christian congregation this may be followed by the attitude of penitence and procrastination: "Almost thou persuadest me to be a Christian. I believe what he says. I'd like to. But not today."[28]

DEVELOPMENT OF DOCTRINAL APPLICATIONS

In developing a specific application, the stress is upon doing. It must be personal, and it must include means and methods. Therefore, the application must be clear to the speaker if it is to be clear to his people in their "being" and "doing" responses.

Applications are to be found within the preacher himself, in the text itself, and from life situations. In the application, the Bible text should be recognized.[29]

Observe general principles. An application may be direct, from past to present. Or it may be indirect through types, inferences, and remarks. An inference is a logical sequence that grows out of the text, whereas a remark is a suggested sequence implied in the text.

Most applications promote decision and change. The use of contrasts in applications can produce a sense of crisis, of hazard, of challenge. Such distress is often a great mind-awakener. The vital alternatives must be life-centered, linked to human wants and needs. Response to any sermon will vary, partly due to the degree of conflict or contrast produced in the message. Contrasts can be effective in calling for a decision.

The main thought in the text will be the main thought in the application. What is not found in the text will not be found in the application. Determine if the call is for direct or indirect application, and include within it an illustration that will illumine the text.

Anticipate audience responses. State clearly the objective response desired from the people, and list ways and means by which to reach the objectives. By writing out the application, concreteness, forcefulness, clarity, and specifics are established.

Application can be employed through silence, emotion, fervor, reverence, and eye-contact. The response of the audience can be seen in three levels: the acceptance level, the belief level, and the action level.

A potentially life-changing application will generally not find fulfillment without the speaker stirring the emotions of the hearer. Garrison finds that to foster a religion of change without making full use of emotional factors in persuasion is like advocating art without beauty and family relationships without affection.[30]

The Word of God has incalculable power in bringing men to the level of action, but often this requires a period of time in which the conviction of the Word and the Holy Spirit are at work.

Consider audience needs. Merrill Abbey suggests five steps in preparing for audience response.

1. Diagnosis. Under this heading the preacher sets down the initials of at least a dozen persons with whom he has had dealings in the pre-

ceding week, setting opposite each some situation or need confronting that individual.

2. Prescription. Reviewing the personal needs he has just listed, he tries to visualize something of what the gospel might bring to each.

3. Exposition. The speaker looks once more at the Scripture on which he has planned to speak . . ., examines it in the light of the needs he has just been facing, inquires what fresh word it has to say to these needs. . . .

4. Experience. The speaker examines himself. "What does this personally mean to me?" "Do I deeply believe it?" "Have I been living it?" "If so, what has it done through me?"

5. Program. The speaker sets down some things he could say to a man who might respond: "That message got me. What do I do now?"[31]

Audience analysis can be pursued through the examination of membership records, interest inventories, questionnaires, and testing. The exposure to the congregation while engaged in pastoral visitation will help in analyzing their attitudes, attachments, and activities. Keep asking, "What is my congregation's present state?" "Where and how far from the present state can they move?" and "At what point does this message touch the lives of people?" John Fritz, in his homiletical refresher course for pastors, encouraged pastoral visitation where the needs of the people can be discovered.[32]

Locate preferred applications. Application will be found in sound exegesis of the biblical text, in a knowledge of the large biblical context of the passage, in an understanding of the historical perspective and of plain common sense, and in the ministry of the Holy Spirit.

The application is found both in the speaker and in the text. The application in the speaker resides in his spirit and manner rather than in any language he employs to express it. It will be conveyed by his sincerity, earnestness, and fidelity to the Word of God. The application is also in the text. The text is chosen because the speaker sees the application in it, and the subject of the text is so announced by the speaker that it contains the application in its initial form.

Use practical illustrations. Application can be made through the use of illustrations. A point well illustrated is a point well taken. Responsibility and response are clarified in this manner. Robert J. McCracken reminds the speaker that the trouble with much preaching is "that it fails either to kindle the mind or to energize the will. It seldom disturbs the conscience or stirs the heart."[33]

Illustrations can be applications or can assist, illumine, clarify, and impress the making of the application. Charles Koller suggests that "the truth may often be more effectively applied . . . by implication than by direct statement. A well chosen illustration is often the most effective means."[34]

Illustrations can serve a number of duties in relationship to application: arouse interest, clarify and make concrete, impress the mind, move the will, convict the apathetic, remove impediments to understanding, stir emotion, bridge the known and unknown, and bridge the accepted and questioned.

Integrate applications appropriately. Applications should be woven into the message in connection with each spiritual truth mentioned. One of the ways of gaining proficiency in this is to make two parallel lists on a sheet of paper. In one the spiritual truth is listed and in the other is listed the possible applications. For practice in developing these applications one could make a list of characteristic human traits and behavior patterns. Beside each of these he could list an appropriate Scripture passage.

Evaluate applications analytically. Homileticians and preachers suggest different criteria to evaluate applications. These standards give helpful guidance for all kinds of sermons but here have special relevance for doctrinal preaching.

1. James Braga writes twenty-one pages on "the application." He lists five prerequisites for effective application.[35]

The preacher must live close to God.

The man of God must be well educated.

The preacher must understand human nature.

The minister must know the conditions and involvements of his people.

There must be complete dependence upon the working of the Spirit of God.

He also lists three basic principles for making messages relevant.

Relate the message to basic human needs and problems.

Make the application specific.

Relate the truth to the times.

Put together, these principles make what is called "interpretive preaching."

2. David Breed included twelve pages on application in his book. His outline contains five points.[36]

Application is in the text and in the subject.

Application is in the man, the preacher.

Application can take various forms.

Application is closely related to what has already been said.

The placement of the application should show variety.

3. H. C. Brown, Jr., lists five factors that influence the correct use of applications.

a) Personal factors of the speaker. The character of the speaker, his knowledge of individuals in the audience, his concern and care for their persons, and his willingness to express warm feelings influence the nature and effectiveness of application in a message.

b) Literary factors of the speaker. This involves the correct use of the elements of speaking and attention given to style. The right word at the right time can have a profound effect.

c) Emotional factors of the speaker. No message can be effective unless it touches emotion and unless it motivates the hearer. In application, the speaker may appeal to those desires and aspirations that assist men to be better men, as well as to reason, fear, obligation, curiosity, and pride.

d) Biblical authority. The speaker who presents biblical truth has biblical authority assisting him in application. He speaks not for himself, the church, or the people; he speaks for God.

e) Divine power. The speaker has divine power assisting him in application. The Holy Spirit takes up the witness to God in self-disclosure and makes the witness understandable and acceptable to the hearer.[37]

The clarity and force of an application can be improved if the following questions are kept in mind during preparation: Is it clear? Is it interesting and significant? Is it vivid? Is it convincing?

Clarify through writing. The preacher should write out the application to be used in the sermon so he may develop clarity of thought and pointedness of direction and focus. An old saying goes, "Conversation makes a ready man, reading makes a full man, and writing makes an exact man."

It is sometimes found to be helpful to write with a definite person in a definite situation before one's mind's eye, asking such questions as these: How would this sound to him? Would he understand it? Would it seem any other than an airy and irrelevant abstraction? During the course of preparation it will also be helpful if the speaker frequently sees himself as the hearer.

Urgency, conviction, and earnestness will characterize the man who has felt the pressure, the burden, the moving of the message in his own heart. "One of the most decisive elements in producing better sermons is that the speaker himself becomes a better Christian."[38] "The pulpit is a mirror held up to the life of the minister. What is in the well of his life will come through the bucket of the pulpit."[39]

The language of application depends upon nouns and pronouns for effectiveness. First and second person pronouns are used for direct, personal application (at times, "we" is used for effectiveness). Words that are indefinite and unnecessary weaken the appeal. Be direct but tactful, straightforward but courteous, all-inclusive but personal. By keeping the individual in focus, it is possible to speak intimately, face to face with each person.

CLASSIFICATION OF DOCTRINAL APPLICATIONS

Three types of application correspond to the three types of doctrinal messages: the declarative application affirms an old truth by bringing it up to date in a dogmatic way, such as would be used in messages on creeds; the apologetic application deals with the relationship of faith to secular knowledge and shows how faith is not at odds with the discoveries of secular man; the polemical application deals with refuting error.

PLACEMENT OF DOCTRINAL APPLICATIONS

The application of the message may come in one of three places: at the end of the sermon, at the end of each main division of the body of the sermon, or at various points throughout the sermon.

At the end of the entire sermon. When the application comes at the end or conclusion of the passage this is known as the compact application. Since the conclusion brings the message to an end and the mind to a decision, the compact application follows the logical arrangement of thought and brings the emotions to a climax. The heart is reached after the mind in informed and convinced by the truth. The conclusion will thus bring the message to a burning climax such as "choose for yourselves today whom you will serve. . . ." (Josh. 24:15).

At the end of each main point. When the application is made at the end of each main point in the body of the message this is known as the divisional application. Each main point or major spiritual truth that supports the proposition of the message must have a point of application. The need for application at each main point grows from the conviction that heavy exposition must be clarified and lightened at various intervals as the attention of the hearer is gained and fixed to each supporting truth of the theme and proposition. This placement of application is helpful in speaking to children or hearers with undisciplined minds.

At many points throughout the entire sermon. When the application is made at numerous places throughout the sermon this is known as the running or continuous application. This was used successfully by George Whitefield whose sermons were directed toward the conscience and did not leave the application to the final few minutes. Many of the Puritan sermons reached their excellence because of the running applications.

THE COMMISSION FOR DOCTRINAL PREACHING

I solemnly charge you in the presence of God and of Christ Jesus, who is to judge the living and the dead, and by His appearing and His kingdom: preach the Word; be ready in season and out of season; reprove, rebuke, exhort, with great patience and instruction. For the time will come when they will not endure sound doctrine; but wanting to have their ears tickled, they will accumulate for themselves teachers in accordance to their own desires; and will turn away their ears from truth, and will turn aside to myths. But you, be sober in all things, endure hardship, do the work of an evangelist, fulfill your ministry. (2 Tim. 4:1-5)

NOTES

1. William Barclay, *The Epistles to Timothy and Titus* (Edinburgh: The Church of Scotland, 1960), p. 77.

2. John H. Jowett, *The Preacher, His Life and Work* (New York: George H. Doran, 1912), pp. 100-101.

3. Charles E. Jefferson, *The Minister as Prophet* (New York: T. Y. Crowell, 1905), chap. 5.

4. Faris D. Whitesell, *The Art of Biblical Preaching* (Grand Rapids: Zondervan, 1950), p. 18.

5. Ibid., p. 45.

6. John Wesley, *Wesley's Standard Sermons* (London: Epworth, 1921), p. 30.

7. David Waite Yohn, *The Contemporary Preacher and His Task* (Grand Rapids: Eerdmans, 1969), pp. 135-36.

8. Andrew Blackwood, *Doctrinal Preaching for Today* (Nashville: Abingdon, 1946), p. 9.

9. Phillips Brooks, *Yale Lectures on Preaching* (New York: Dutton, 1879), p. 129.

10. J. M. Reu, *Homiletics: A Manual of the Theory and Practice of Preaching* (Grand Rapids: Baker, 1967), pp. 151, 153.

11. Gerald Judd, *Crisis in the Church* (Philadelphia: Pilgrim, 1968), pp. 46-47.

12. Corwin Roach, *Preaching Values in the Bible* (Louisville, Ky.: Cloister, 1946), p. 125.

13. Ezekiel Robinson, *Lectures on Preaching* (New York: Henry Holt, 1883), pp. 165-66.

14. James Black, *The Mystery of Preaching* (New York: Revell, 1924), p. 105.

15. J. Winston Pearce, *Planning Your Preaching* (Nashville: Broadman, 1967), p. 74.

16. Robinson, *Lectures on Preaching,* p. 163.

17. James Hoppin, *Homiletics* (New York: Funk and Wagnalls, 1883), p. 689.

18. R. C. Lenski, *The Sermon: Its Homiletical Construction* (Grand Rapids: Baker, 1968), p. 228.

19. John Wood, *The Preacher's Workshop* (Chicago: InterVarsity, 1965), p. 43.

20. A. W. Tozer, *Of God and Men* (Harrisburg, Pa.: Christian Publications, 1960), pp. 26-27.

21. H. C. Brown Jr., *A Quest for Reformation in Preaching* (Waco, Tex.: Word, 1968), p. 60.

22. Tozer, *Of God and Men,* p. 27.

23. David James Burrell, *The Sermon: Its Construction and Delivery* (New York: Revell, 1913), p. 76.

24. Faris D. Whitesell, *Power in Expository Preaching* (Westwood, N.J.: Revell, 1963), pp. 91-102.

25. Ibid.

26. Hoppin, *Homiletics,* p. 689.

27. James Stalker, *The Preacher and His Models* (Grand Rapids: Baker, 1967), p. 256.

28. Ambrose Moody Bailey, *Stand Up and Preach* (New York: Round Table, 1937), pp. 79-80.

29. Reu, *Homiletics,* p. 362.

30. Webb Garrison, *The Preacher and His Audience* (Westwood, N.J.: Revell, 1954), p. 229.

31. Merrill Abbey, *Living Doctrine in a Vital Pulpit* (New York: Abingdon, 1964), pp. 45-49.

32. John Fritz, *Essentials of Preaching: A Refresher Course in Homiletics for Pastors* (St. Louis: Concordia, 1948), pp. 54-61.

33. Robert J. McCracken, *The Making of a Sermon* (New York: Harper, 1956), p. 18.

34. Charles W. Koller, *Expository Preaching Without Notes* (Grand Rapids: Baker, 1962), p. 51.

35. James Braga, *How to Prepare Bible Messages* (Portland: Multnomah, 1971), pp. 173-94.

36. David R. Breed, *Preparing to Preach* (New York: George H. Doran, 1911), pp. 273-83.

37. Brown, *A Quest for Reformation in Preaching,* pp. 63-64.

BIBLIOGRAPHY

Abbey, Merrill R. *Living Doctrines in a Vital Pulpit.* Nashville: Abingdon, 1965.

Baker, Eric. *Preaching Theology.* London: Epworth, 1954.

Barth, Karl. *The Preaching of the Gospel.* Philadelphia: Westminster, 1963.

* Blackwood, Andrew W. *Doctrinal Preaching for Today.* New York: Abingdon-Cokesbury, 1956.

Carl, William J., III. *Preaching Christian Doctrine.* Philadelphia: Fortress, 1973.

Clowney, Edmund. *Preaching and Biblical Theology.* Grand Rapids: Eerdmans, 1961.

Demaray, Donald E. *Proclaiming the Truth.* Grand Rapids: Baker, 1979.

McCracken, Robert J. *The Making of the Sermon.* New York: Harper, 1956.

Randolph, David James. *The Renewal of Preaching.* Philadelphia: Fortress, 1969.

* Reu, J. M. *Homiletics: A Manual of the Theory and Practice of Preaching.* Chicago: Wartburg, 1922.

Stevenson, Dwight. *In the Biblical Preacher's Workshop.* Nashville: Abingdon, 1967.

Stott, John. *Between Two Worlds: The Art of Preaching in the Twentieth Century.* Grands Rapids: Eerdmans, 1982.

* Sweeting, George. *Special Sermons on Major Bible Doctrines.* Chicago: Moody, 1981.

Thompson, William D. *Preaching Biblically.* Nashville: Abingdon, 1981.

von Allmen, Jean Jacques. *Preaching and Congregation.* Richmond: John Knox, 1962.

8

BIBLICAL PREACHING AND EVANGELISTIC MESSAGES

> Too much so-called evangelistic preaching has been shal-
> low, partisan, and emotional without much thought content.
> (Faris D. Whitesell, *Evangelistic Preaching and the Old Testament*
> [Chicago: Moody, 1947], p. 34)

So lamented Faris Whitesell more than forty years ago. Today, as
then, the great need of the hour is exposition in evangelism. The
evangelistic preacher must have something to say to a dying world.
The Word of God must be as a fire burning in his soul. His mind and
heart must be filled with the biblical text.

He must work with the text with toil and tears, allowing it to
take hold in his own experience and then through the power of the
Holy Spirit become an agent in changing the lives of searching people. He must work with the original languages of the text (if at all
possible), seek to appreciate the history and culture of the biblical
writer, and try to respond to the original author's intention with
cogent applications that make their mark. Only then will the evangelistic sermon be biblically accurate, intellectually stimulating, relevant, and spiritually transforming.

THE NEED FOR EVANGELISTIC MESSAGES

The church needs evangelism to save herself from the sterility of
a merely cultural religion. The life of the church and her hope for
the future lie in her reproductive power, which is evangelism. The
local congregation must evangelize or die.

Some churches seem to belong to the cult of the comfortable.
They seem to have become satisfied with themselves. They are
neglecting their outreach responsibilities and are thus missing great
privileges. Churches grow and are especially blessed when high priority is given to effective evangelism.

The word is out among some pastors, church leaders, seminary professors, and ministerial students that evangelistic preaching does not work anymore. Some suggest that in our different world of today only inner city reclamation, discussion groups, world-awareness studies, renewal of liturgy, and other kinds of "modern" ministry can be used to call people to God. It is the conviction of the author of this book, however, that biblical evangelistic preaching can still be a very effective means of reaching souls for the Savior.

The time has come for a revival atmosphere to be created by the Holy Spirit in the churches of our land. When individuals get "on fire for God," the unsaved will be prompted to come and see them "burn." The health curve of the church across the centuries can be traced in accordance with the evangelistic fervor in the pulpits. The church must have the same burden as her Lord, of whom it was declared, "[He came] to seek and to save that which was lost" (Luke 19:10).

THE DESCRIPTIONS OF EVANGELISTIC MESSAGES

THEY ARE DESCRIBED BY ESSENTIALS

Bible-based. The biblical text must be the foundation of every evangelistic sermon. The evangelist must specialize in the publication of the message of the gospel. Whereas in a lecture, the subject dominates everything, in the evangelistic sermon, the man speaking is so central that in a certain sense the sermon is the man. Therefore, in order for the evangelistic sermon to be truly Bible-based, the truth must pass through the life of the preacher. The preacher's life interprets and enforces that truth. The biblical text must grip the preacher and stir his heart before he can hope to stir the imagination and prod the conscience of the hearer.

People-centered. The evangelistic sermon must be directed accurately toward the hearer and at life as it is being lived today. The evangelistic sermon must be aimed at convincing the hearer's mind, moving his feelings, and persuading his will to the point at which he will accept as his philosophy of life, "For to me to live is Christ, and to die is gain" (Phil. 1:21).

THEY ARE DESCRIBED BY LEADERS

In the history of homiletics, evangelistic preaching has been described in various terms.

Revivalistic preaching. Originally, revivalistic preaching was the term in vogue. Early works dealing with evangelistic preaching, such as John Kern's *The Ministry of the Congregation* (1897), J. A. Broadus's *On the Preparation and Delivery of Sermons* (revised 1898), and John Etter's *The Preacher and His Sermon* (1891), employed this terminology. According to Etter, who wrote nineteen pages on the subject, revivalistic preaching has a twofold emphasis, namely, to convert the sinner and to revive the saints.[1]

Soul-winning preaching. Later, the term soul-winning preaching became the label for evangelistic preaching. Frederick E. Taylor devoted thirty pages to soul-winning preaching in his book *The Evangelistic Church* (1927). He suggested that if such preaching is to be effective, it must be prayerful, positive, practical, personal, and persuasive.[2] Andrew Blackwood, the famed homilist and pastoral theologian at Princeton Theological Seminary, characterized soul-winning preaching as biblical in substance, doctrinal in form, and popular in style. More specifically he said, "The sermon that saves the soul brings the hearer face to face with the Son of God and moves him to accept Jesus as Savior and Lord. In every soul-winning message there is a note of urgency, 'Now is the accepted.'"[3]

Gospel-publishing. Taylor was a contemporary of Ozora S. Davis. Davis defined evangelistic sermons as "those sermons which were designed primarily to publish the gospel as a message to those who never had heard it or who needed to hear some new aspects of it presented."[4]

Decision-oriented. Whitesell definitively described evangelistic preaching as "preaching at its best." He said:

> It is preaching adapted to the highest ends of the gospel—turning men from sin and darkness to salvation and light. Evangelistic preaching is preaching with a mission—an immediate and all-important mission—winning a verdict in favor of the Lord Jesus Christ. The evangelistic sermon is an all-out effort to bring the lost to Christ. A devotional or inspirational sermon, with an evangelistic kite-tail attached, is not an evangelistic sermon. A sermon with a mild evangelistic strain or color running through it is not an evangelistic sermon. These sermons may be good and perfectly appropriate for many occasions, but such preaching ought not to be called evangelistic preaching. The true evangelistic sermon is a *planned, organized and concentrated drive toward the goal of decisions for Christ* [emphasis added].[5]

The emphasis on a drive toward a decision has become a hallmark of evangelistic preaching and has expressed itself even in the new terminology employed for evangelistic preaching—kerygmatic preaching.

Kerygmatic preaching. H. C. Brown, Jr., employed the term *kerygmatic* to describe evangelistic preaching. He defined the evangelistic objective by explaining, "Men are saved by hearing the gospel preached or explained and by committing themselves to Jesus Christ."[6]

In 1972, J. Daniel Baumann, formerly the department chairman of pastoral ministries and director of field education at Bethel Theological Seminary, wrote a book entitled *An Introduction to Contemporary Preaching.* Said Dr. Baumann, "Kerygmatic preaching is also called proclamation or evangelistic preaching. . . . Proclamation is unashamed evangelistic preaching that calls man to make a personal decision regarding Jesus Christ as Savior and Lord."[7]

Preaching involves presenting Jesus Christ in such a manner that men and women may come to know Him, love Him, serve Him and yield their lives completely to Him. Such definitions as these emphasize that the gospel is to be presented so that the hearer will understand its implications and be brought to the place of decision for Christ.

THE POWER OF EVANGELISTIC MESSAGES

To preach in the energy of the flesh is to be utterly fruitless. Paul was well aware of this when he wrote to the Thessalonians, "For our gospel did not come to you in word only, but also in power and in the Holy Spirit and with full conviction" (1 Thess. 1:5). Evangelists do not dare to depend on natural means to produce supernatural results.

The Holy Spirit calls and equips the evangelists, and He also strengthens them for this monumental task. The Spirit of God enables the preacher to discipline his mind and body. He prods the man of God to deeper devotional study and intercessory prayer. He helps him handle the multiplicity of demands on his time and energy that otherwise would inhibit and stunt his ministry and influence for Christ.

The strategic role of the Holy Spirit in the sermonizer's preparation is seen in the ministries He performs. The Holy Spirit is the producer of the evangelist's primary source material, the Word of God. He is the penetrator of the evangelist's understanding, enabling him to properly observe, interpret, apply, and communicate gospel truth. He is the provider of the evangelist's authority. Apart from the divine truth internalized through the indwelling presence and illumination of the Spirit of God, there is no authority in evangelistic preaching.

THE STYLE OF EVANGELISTIC MESSAGES

THE IMPORTANCE OF EVANGELISTIC STYLE

For widest possible understanding. Style was an important asset to the evangelists who made their mark in the history of preaching. Two key evangelists especially known for their style were John Wesley and Charles G. Finney. As mentioned in the previous chapter, Wesley studiously avoided "all words which are not easy to be understood, and all which are not used in common life."[8] Finney's style coincided to a great degree with Wesley's in that he, too, ignored the religious terminology of the schools of higher learning, choosing rather to couch his sermons in the homely and everyday terms of the common man.

For greatest possible response. The importance of good sermonic style, especially with reference to the evangelistic sermon, cannot be overemphasized. It was said of Henry Clay that he made his friends with one vocabulary and lost the presidency with another. Likewise an evangelist can lose his congregation if he is not careful to develop a lucid and articulate style that crosses all the communication barriers confronting him in any given evangelistic setting. To lose the audience, in the case of evangelistic sermons, is to lose souls.

To develop such a style, the preacher, as he sits at his desk preparing his sermon, must ever keep in mind the nature of the people he is addressing. He must write as he is going to speak, going over the language he uses time and again to make sure that each thought is clear, understandable, and unambiguous. As he pours over the style of his sermon, he must see to it that each word means to his audience what it means to him; if one does not, he must readily substitute for it a more accurate word.

This exacting attention to style is for the blessing of people and the glory of God. The greater the simplicity and motivation of evangelistic messages, the greater the understanding; the greater the understanding, the greater the response. The salvation of souls for the worship and glory of God is the ultimate rationale for this concern with style.

The evangelist who is concerned with style would do well to heed the admonition of T. L. Cuyler when he said, "Begin to preach in such a style that you shall nail every ear to the pulpit; end your discourse with an appeal that shall clench the truth and send your hearer home with God's Word ringing in his memory."[9]

Accuracy of expression. Improvement of style should be one of the goals of every evangelistic preaching experience. "Status quo-itis" should be fought off. Development and improvement ought to be uppermost in the preacher's mind. An evangelist can perfect his style by avoiding the use of slang language and slipshod English. Charles Templeton put this principle in perspective: "The goal is not accommodation to the linguistic practice of a generation but statement in terms that have meaning to the hearer."[10]

Restraint of expression. Improvement also comes to evangelistic style when concise diction is used. In regard to this, Louis Brastow's words are appropriate: "One needs to know not only what to say, but how much and when and where, and how to stop. The adequate evangelistic sermon carries no surplus material. It eliminates padding. It wastes no words. It is dangerous to say too much. He who speaks to the feelings of his hearers may easily cause a revulsion. A little overdoing spoils the impression."[11]

From a different viewpoint, evangelistic style can be enhanced by getting right to the main point of the message without camouflaging the real intent with anecdotes and niceties that distract the hearer, keeping him from hearing what he came to hear, namely, the gospel of Christ presented in a plain and effective manner.

Mutuality of expression. The use of nontechnical language will also immediately improve evangelistic style. As has been noted already, the use of such language was one of Finney's main strengths. He exhorted his readers to use the "language of the common life." That is, the evangelist should use words that the members of the congregation know well and use frequently. A technical term—even if it is explained at the beginning of the sermon—is bound to be forgotten, and ultimately it can confuse people who do not usually remember the special meanings that an evangelist may attach to certain words. Finney further warned:

> If [an evangelist]uses a word in common use, but employs it in an uncommon sense, giving his special explanations, it is no better; for the people will soon forget his special explanations, and then the impression actually conveyed to their minds will be according to their common understanding of the word. And thus he will never convey the right idea to his congregation.[12]

Repetition of expression. The purposeful repetition of ideas can also provide improvement in the evangelist's style. To repeat key thoughts and phrases for emphasis is not a weakness but a strength. Effective repetition was one of the distinctive features characterizing the style of radio evangelist Walter A. Maier. He often repeated not only key concepts, but also imperative verbs that contributed significant insights into the biblical text. Between such repetitions he interspersed life-related facts and relevant ideas gleaned from a wide range of reading.

Visualization in expression. Henry Sloane Coffin suggested that the preacher can improve his style by employing language that enables the congregation to visualize what he is saying.

> The preacher will try for language which makes his hearers see. All words of art—and a sermon is one of the highest forms of literary creation—awaken the imagination. A moving speaker turns men's ears into eyes. They are made to see life's situations, and situations which lie in the realm of the spirit, and made to feel themselves in them. The language which a preacher wants is that of novelists and poets and dramatists, and of writers of letters and of autobiography, who capture and exhibit the workings of the mind and heart. He has to avoid the abstract, and for this reason he must rid himself not only of the jargon of theological lecture rooms and of most of his scholarly books, but also of their unimaginative way of putting things. He must shun such prosaic and pedestrian forms and expressions as these lectures are cast in.[13]

THE QUALITIES OF EVANGELISTIC STYLE

Several qualities should characterize the style of the effective evangelistic sermon. Each quality comes as the result of work on the part of the sermonizer who sees the phrasing of words as an integral part of the sermonic process.

Naturalness. First, the evangelistic sermon should be natural. The sermonizer should not seek to imitate the evangelistic style of another preacher. Natural style helped to make Spurgeon, Moody, Finney, and Whitefield great evangelists. Said Brastow: "There is nothing in the discourses of these great evangelists that insures their perpetuity. But they express what is real to them, and they bear the evidence of reality in their directness and pungency. A religious awakening is likely to bring a revival of naturalness, simplicity, directness, compactness and cogency of speech."[14]

Simplicity. Effective evangelistic style is also known for its simplicity. Some think that simplicity of style renders an evangelistic sermon easy to formulate. Said Charles Goodell, "If one thinks that simple, soulful words are easily spoken, and that they are the sign of lack of preparation, let him try to use them, and he will discern his mistake."[15] Coffin reminded the sermonizer: "We have to paint life's occurrences as that our hearers seem to themselves to be living through them. We have to take out of their mouths the phrases they use."[16]

To be simple does not mean to be juvenile or unacademic. A simple style does not employ hackneyed expressions. Simplicity of style means that the sermon is couched in such terminology that even the uneducated can understand and respond to the message of the gospel.

Familiarity. Life-relatedness is a third important quality of evangelistic style that must be developed. The language the preacher employs should be contemporary and readily recognizable by the average man or woman. The phraseology used should be in terms of present needs and problems. Jesus Himself used a language of life that confronted people where they were and then awakened positive response. The people always knew what He was talking about because He used a terminology that was familiar to them.

Clarity. Evangelistic style should be clear and understandable. It is said that W. E. Sangster liked the inspired misquotation, "Though I speak with the tongues of men and angels and have not clarity, I am become as sounding brass and tinkling cymbal." Albert Barnes rightly asserted, "The hopes of the Gospel are so clear that there is no need of ambiguity or enigma; no need of abstruse metaphysical reasoning in the pulpit."[17]

A clear style omits all irrelevancies and speculations that have no direct bearing on the subject at hand. A sermon that is not clear is of no use to the people in the congregation. In fact, a sermon that is not understandable is really an indictment against the preacher. James Porter said, "Strange and obscure terms in the pulpit argue more for the pride and conceit of the minister, than for his piety or good taste. They strongly indicate that the conversion of the people is not his object, or that he is deficient in judgment."[18]

Again, a clear style does not employ Greek and Latin phrases that may seem, from the evangelist's point of view, to put the academic stamp on the message, but that only confuse the congregation. Finney said that he had heard some revivalistic preachers whose language was so far over the heads of the people that if the latter had not come equipped with dictionaries, they would not have understood at all. Of such an obscure style he said, "So many phrases were brought in, manifestly to adorn the discourse, rather than to instruct the people that I have felt as if I wanted to tell the man, 'Sit down and not confound the people's mind with your *barbarian* preaching, that they cannot understand.'"[19]

Personality. Cultivating a personal style will also be advantageous for the evangelistic preacher. Jesse Burton Weatherspoon, in his *Sent Forth to Preach,* said that this was especially demonstrated in the apostolic, evangelistic preaching of Peter, Stephen, and Paul. What they preached represented their personal beliefs as based upon the revealed Word of God, and their sermons were often openly autobiographical. This quality of style, however, must not be abused. Such abuse arises when the preacher sets himself up as a worthy personal example to follow. Nevertheless, personal experience, used with discretion, can be very effective.

Intelligence. The evangelistic preacher should seek to develop an educational style. He must appeal not only to the emotions but also to the mind of the listener. This can be done in a clear and understandable manner. Paul S. Rees in *Stir Up the Gift* was right in labeling as fallacy the assertion that evangelism and education are incompatible.

Empathy. The empathetic quality is also an important aspect of evangelistic style. Not only should the preacher have his hearers before him as he prepares, but he should also put himself "in their shoes." How would he respond if he were in the pew rather than in the pulpit? An empathetic style makes for a sympathetic audience. People will respond more readily if the preacher's words let them know that he has been in their situation.

Rapport. An animated, or conversational, style is a key quality in evangelistic preaching. Being able to converse with one's audience rather than just talk at them is a noble quality. In our day, Billy Graham evidences such a conversational quality, especially in his use of rhetorical questions. It is interesting that a conversational style was promoted by Finney even though many of his predecessors were opposed to it. Said Finney:

> [Style] should be conversational. Preaching to be understood should be colloquial in its style. A minister must preach just as he would talk, if he wishes to be fully understood. Nothing is more calculated to make a sinner feel that religion is some mysterious thing that he cannot understand, than this mouthing, formal, lofty style of speaking so generally employed in the pulpit. The minister ought to do as the lawyer does when he wants to make a jury understand him perfectly. He uses a style perfectly colloquial. This lofty, swelling style will do no good. The gospel will never produce any great effects, until ministers talk to their hearers, in the pulpit, as they talk in private conversation.[20]

Morality. Henry Sloane Coffin said that evangelistic style is partly a moral quality: "[It is] a resolve to portray what one feels so that one's hearers feel it, an abnegation of slovenly and slipshod diction, a refusal to clutter up sentences with phrases which do not stand for actualities, a passion for the exact and comely word. And it is partly a gift of the imagination, bestowed in varying measures, sometimes dulled and sometimes enhanced by culture."[21]

Bible. Style should also be biblical. That is, the preacher should not be afraid to use biblical terminology in his sermon. It is interesting to note that Finney expressed the same concern that many present-day preachers and theologians are expressing about technical biblical words and phrases such as *regeneration* and *sanctification*; namely, they are often alluded to but seldom defined. The only way to help people understand technical biblical terms is to define and explain them when they are employed in any given evangelistic sermon. Rather than avoiding the use of biblical words and theological concepts, the effective evangelist will employ them sparingly, explaining them in everyday terminology and using some pertinent, life-related illustrations.

Boldness. Evangelistic style should be direct and fearless. Andrew Blackwood observed: "The man in the pulpit is no mere essayist who has been rambling about in a garden and plucking beautiful flowers so as to bedeck the Cross. He is an ambassador from King Christ, with a message that calls for decision, here and now. Would the ambassador from the Court of Saint James tone down the words of his monarch? No! In like manner, without being abrupt or tactless, the soul-winning preacher addresses the man in the pew."[22]

Urgency. Finally, urgency should be evident in evangelistic style. As one clothes his sermon with words, he should endeavor to win the wills of his audience. This may be accomplished by appealing either to the intellect or to the emotions. Again, Blackwood is helpful:

> As a rule the first portion of the message is chiefly to the intellect; the latter part may be more to the emotions. But in the fine art of preaching all our rules break down. The main thing is to have a message from God and then preach it with a soul on fire. According to Father Taylor, the evangelist to seamen, the preacher must "take something hot out of his own heart and shove it into mine."[23]

THE PERSUASION IN EVANGELISTIC MESSAGES

In its generic sense, persuasion is any verbal method of influencing human conduct. In its specific meaning, persuasion refers to influencing human conduct by emotional appeals. It is instilling, activating, or directing in another individual a belief or type of conduct recommended by the speaker. This process involves logic, emotion, and ethics.

It is important that the evangelist recognize the type of audience to which he is presenting the evangelistic message. The methods employed in persuasion will vary with the type of audience to which he presents his message.

There are four types of audiences in terms of their interests and their attitude toward the speaker and the ideas included in his presentation. These four audiences are the apathetic, doubting, hostile, and believing.

The first reaction might be to question presenting the evangelistic message to that fourth audience type, the believing audience. David Breed in his work *Preparing to Preach* stated that the evangelistic sermon should be preached to the entire congregation. Some will be aroused; some will be convicted. But all will be helped, stimulated, and comforted.

The evangelist may misjudge the spiritual status of some of his audience. He might personally tend to classify them as believers whereas in reality they might not be. The typical audience will have representatives from all four types of listeners. The evangelistic preacher gains several distinct advantages by carefully analyzing his audience. He can make his appeal more direct and meaningful if he knows the background, difficulties, and trials of his hearers.

PERSUADING THE APATHETIC AUDIENCE

The apathetic audience is one that is not interested in the message. The members of it do not believe, oppose, or doubt the presentation. They just don't have any interest in it.

The physical factors in the speaking situation take on special significance when such an audience is involved. Some of these factors will be outside the control of the speaker, whereas there will be others he may alter, providing he is aware of the need and the possible methods for improvement.

It will be helpful to polarize the audience. This can be done by having them seated close together. They should be encouraged to enter into joint participation in laughing, singing, and sharing. If the speaker emphasizes near the beginning, matters on which the audience has common agreement, such will tend to draw the audience together. Stress should be placed upon the unanimity of feeling that exists among the auditors.

Distractions should be removed from the speaking area. A concentration of light should be centered upon the speaker. This light should be located so that it does not reflect upon glasses and should be of such coloring that it does not give a sallow complexion to the speaker. Do not dim the lights in the congregation during the message. It is imperative that the speaker see his audience in order to sense their reaction to elements in his message. This will help him capture attention, maintain interest, and persuade them.

A high speaking platform will work to the disadvantage of the speaker. Such a platform will encourage the audience to doze while the speaker is delivering the message. This is due partly to the fact that the eyes will be encouraged to roll upward and backward as when one sleeps.

The correct temperature level and proper ventilation are two important factors. The temperature level should be set at about sixty-eight degrees before the audience arrives. It will then lift to a height of about seventy-two degrees during the message.

Any motor activity on the part of the speaker helps to get the attention of the audience. There are some guides, however, that should be followed. The speaker should not rush to the lectern and begin speaking immediately. It is better to approach the speaking location in a poised manner. He should then stand for just a moment before beginning to speak. It is normally wise to avoid gestures in the introduction. Avoid activity that merely indicates the nervous condition of the speaker but does not enhance the presentation of the message.

The first few minutes of a message are of special importance. It is wise to avoid big, abstract generalizations, a long, rambling history of the subject or the exposition of the background of knowledge that will be necessary for the understanding of your message. This includes overelaborate preliminaries and definitions. Do not begin with an apology. As a rule, one should avoid the routine beginning of giving all the message away in the introduction.

An effective introduction will be short, presented with quiet confidence, and characterized by variation in delivery. The following ideas and types of material are helpful in gaining and holding attention. Relevant humorous material and that which is novel or unusual gets attention. People have a tendency to listen to material pertaining to familiar homely doings. Action and conflict material maintains interest. Listeners have a tendency to pay attention to human interest material such as eccentricities of all kinds. Heart interest material such as stories of struggles, defeats, and victories have special appeal.

PERSUADING THE DOUBTING AUDIENCE

The doubting audience is one that has not as yet formed definite opinions. They need to see the weight of the data. It is necessary to show the validity of the argument itself without injecting too much of the personality of the speaker. The speaker must be able to talk factually, make predictions, develop theories, and draw logical conclusions. General semantics, which involves a study of language, facts, and human evaluations, has made valuable contributions in this area of speaking factually. The speaker should not present inferences as though they were fact.

It is important to remember that, when we are dealing with people, all situations present complexities. No two people are alike, and consequently their actions cannot be predicted with certainty.

There is a tendency in English to overemphasize similarities and overlook differences. We thus distort the pictures of the world in which we live and make it difficult to see variety as it exists. In dealing with the doubtful audience we should strive to fix the variables by giving the specifics of identification.

It is not only important to talk factually with a doubtful audience, but it is also important to be able to make predictions. It is important that the preacher be able to satisfy the tests of authority if he wants the listener to rely upon his predictions. It is not enough to say that someone stated it, and therefore, it must be true.

PERSUADING THE HOSTILE AUDIENCE

When a speaker is dealing with a hostile audience, it is helpful to develop a response to the speaker as a person. This involves establishing his authority to speak. The speaker's force, vitality, poise, and confidence will go far in establishing one's authority. His sincerity, sympathy, kindness, and compassion will enhance the presentation.

The speaker should show respect for the audience by not being too pompous and patronizing, nor should he be too deferential and obsequious. He should avoid habitual overstatements and avoid cultivating a pattern of understatements.

The speaker in his approach to the hostile audience may emphasize all of the areas in which he as a speaker and the audience have common interests. He may begin his message by asking a series of questions to which the audience will give quiet assent within their minds. He may approach the audience with absolute candor where he will state his purposes openly.

PERSUADING THE BELIEVING AUDIENCE

The believing audience is often a passive audience. It accepts the position of the speaker but just does not respond to his pleas for acceptance and action.

The presentation to such an audience should contain a maximum of illustrations and a minimum of principles. The speaker may make use of visual aids since theoretically every idea can be visualized. He may want to invite audience participation. Illustrations such as anecdotes and examples will reduce fatigue. Without examples principles really make no sense. The speaker will find it profitable to use comparisons, similes, and metaphors. It is helpful to include the telling details. These are the little details the average person would tend to overlook.

THE INVITATIONS IN EVANGELISTIC MESSAGES

The emphasis upon the drive for a decision has become a hallmark of evangelistic preaching and has expressed itself even in the new terminology employed for evangelistic preaching—*kerygmatic* preaching. This term is used by J. C. Brown, Jr., in his book *A Quest for Reformation in Preaching* to describe evangelistic preaching.

DEFINITION OF EVANGELISTIC INVITATIONS

The evangelistic sermon has been known primarily by the invitation that often accompanies it. Definitively, the sermonic invitation is that part of the message that issues a challenge to the congregation to act positively upon what the preacher has proclaimed from the Word of God.

J. Daniel Baumann, quoting Clifton J. Allen, offered this definition: "The invitation is not a gimmick to catch souls. It is not a fetish to insure results. It is not a ritual to confirm orthodoxy. It is simply the call of Christ to confront persons with the offer of his redemption, the demands of his lordship, and the privilege of his service."[24]

IMPORTANCE OF EVANGELISTIC INVITATIONS

Ozora Davis expressed the sentiments of almost all the writers in the field of evangelistic and homiletic theory when he said: "The most important factor . . . in the evangelistic sermon is the direct drive for a decision in favor of the message on the part of the hearers."[25] The importance of an invitation was expressed by Leighton Ford: "I am convinced that the giving of some kind of public invitation to come to Christ is not only theologically correct, but also emotionally sound. Men need this opportunity for expression. The inner decision for Christ is like driving a nail through a board. The open declaration of it is like clinching the nail on the other side, so that it is not easily pulled out. Impression without expression can lead to depression."[26]

REASONS FOR EVANGELISTIC INVITATIONS

They are biblically based. There are many reasons for giving evangelistic invitations. First, an appropriate invitation is biblical. Our Lord Himself uttered pleadingly, "Come to Me, all who are weary and heavy-laden, and I will give you rest. Take My yoke upon you, and learn from Me, for I am gentle and humble in heart: and you shall find rest for your souls" (Matt. 11:28-29). The New Testament record closes with a great invitation: "And the Spirit and the bride say, 'Come.' And let the one who hears say, 'Come.' And let the one who is thirsty come; let the one who wishes take the water of life without cost" (Rev. 22:17).

The Old Testament prophets also pressed for a decision. Hosea, in pleading for the people of the Lord to return to Him and accept His forgiving grace, said, "Take words with you and return to the Lord: say to Him, 'Take away all iniquity, and receive us graciously'" (Hos. 14:2).

The prophet Isaiah appealed to his hearers' intellectual and reasoning powers in declaring that God would help the sincere sinner think through his need of redemption: "'Come now, and let us reason together,' says the Lord, 'Though your sins are as scarlet, they will be as white as snow; though they are red like crimson, they will be like wool'" (Isa. 1:18).

They are psychologically sound. Evangelistic invitations are psychological. Faris Whitesell explained, "Emotions aroused and desires stirred will soon pass away unless acted upon at once. Good impulses are harder to generate the second time than they were the first time if the first impulse did not result in action."[27]

They are historically proved. An evangelistic invitation has been a historically proved method of bringing men to Christ. Almost without exception, the great evangelistic preachers, both past and present, have used some form of invitation in securing the results of their messages.

PROBLEMS WITH EVANGELISTIC INVITATIONS

There are three problems involved in calling for a public decision. The first is the theological issue. Leighton Ford has pointed out that two outstanding evangelical preachers, the late Dr. Donald Grey Barnhouse and Dr. Martyn Lloyd-Jones, avoided public decision making, considering it to be inconsistent with the doctrines of man's inability, grace, and God's election.[28]

The second problem is the emotional issue. Dr. Ford believes that one must distinguish between emotionalism and emotion: "Emotionalism is emotion isolated. It involves the use of emotions for emotion's sake. There is a legitimate place for emotion in preaching the gospel. Nothing truly human lacks emotion."[29] Although emotions are vitally important, one must appeal to the whole man—intellect, conscience, emotions, and will (see Mark 12:30).

The third problem in giving an invitation is the practical one.

This issue involves the danger, on the one hand, of having no method of bringing people to Christ, and the opposite danger of overusing one method to the point of "boxing up" and limiting the Holy Spirit in our preconceived practices.

VARIATIONS OF EVANGELISTIC INVITATIONS

There are many different kinds, or variations, of invitation that the preacher can use.

The age-group invitation. Here the evangelist in advance selects various people within the congregation who have come to Christ at different ages—age ten, fifteen, twenty, and so on.

The altar-call invitation. The song leader leads the congregation in an invitatory hymn while the evangelist pleads with people to come to Christ. People are encouraged to come forward and kneel at the altar, where other Christians deal with them.

The Christians-lead-the-way invitation. The evangelist asks Christians to come forward and pray for the unconverted. As they pray, the unsaved are asked to respond.

The contact-the-pastor invitation. The evangelist invites the people who have been helped by the message to contact the pastor, either at the close of the service or during the week, to talk over their decision for Christ or to receive more counsel.

The decision-within-the-heart invitation. This is made quite apart from any outward display and is usually implicit in the closing prayer, wherein the preacher asks the Lord to help the people practice the truth of the message during the coming week.

The discussion-and-debate invitation. This was the method of Dr. James Reid, who invited his congregation to the hall in his church after an evangelistic sermon to encourage dialogue about the message. Both the saved and the unsaved could ask questions and exchange ideas.

The inquiry-room invitation. The evangelist invites all who want to make a commitment to Christ to come forward so that they can be directed to an adjoining room for prayer and spiritual counsel by trained leaders.

The pray-it-through invitation. The evangelist asks for no visible response but exhorts those who have been deeply touched to go home and think and pray over the message until they have made their peace with God.

The raised-hands invitation. Just before he closes the meeting in prayer, the evangelist asks all those whose hearts have been touched by the Holy Spirit to raise their hands for prayer. He then prays, asking God to help them obey the message and respond to Christ.

The sign-the-card invitation. In this case, the people in the congregation are urged to sign a card, indicating the kind of decision they have made, and hand it to the pastor as they leave the service. The evangelist can then follow up on those who handed in cards.

The standing invitation. Those who have made decisions for Christ are invited to stand as a silent witness to their newfound faith.

PERSUASION IN EVANGELISTIC INVITATIONS

It should be carefully planned. The invitation, to be persuasive, must be tied in closely with the major thrust of the sermon. In other words, it should be carefully planned and written out. It should grow out of the main theme of the message so that the people will not be surprised when it is given. People should know exactly why they are responding. Consequently, if one's sermonic emphasis is on the salvation of sinners, the invitation will be directed toward the lost. If the thrust is on Christian stewardship with reference to time, talents, and treasure, the invitation should challenge the people to tithe and give of their time and talents to the service of the Lord.

Persuasion is accomplished not only through letting the invitation grow out of the sermon, but also through purposefully choosing the content of the message. To do this, one must preach on the great and moving themes of the Bible. The preacher must vividly confront unbelievers with the illogic of their position by pointing out on one hand the results of sin and, on the other hand, the resources and power they can have through faith in Christ. He must point out that God cannot be eluded indefinitely and that only Christ can make the guilty guiltless. He must hold up Christ as the All-Sufficient One and make the cross the center of his appeal.

It can be widely varied. Persuasion is also accomplished by being aware of the various appeals that move people. Charles Koller listed seven appeals, or roads, to the heart. These include the appeals to altruism, aspiration, curiosity, duty, fear, love, and reason.

George Sweazey enlarged on that number by suggesting twenty evangelistic appeals. These included appeals to the sense of sin, dread of impersonal forces, lost assurances, anxiety, boredom, self-perplexity, death, loneliness, the sense of something lacking, hunger for truth, the missing significance of God, mistrust of life, inner conflict, resentment of material domination, eagerness for a better world, the appeal to the heroic, the craving for brotherhood, love of home and family, admiration for Jesus Christ, and the power of the cross.[30] To these appeals, V. L. Stanfield added the appeals to the basic drives inherent to individuals, such as self-preservation, personal happiness, recognition or prestige, security, freedom, adventure, and satisfaction.[31]

It must be appropriately timed. A factor often overlooked in a consideration of persuasiveness is the time factor involved. That is, when is the best time for making the appeal to act on the truth of the message? The best time is at the conclusion of the message, when people are still in their seats, not while they are standing, reaching for the hymnbooks, taking care of the children, and, in general, getting ready to bolt for the exits. The reason for this is obvious. Only when the evangelist has the undivided attention of the audience can his invitation be persuasive and well understood. If there is much disturbance, the people in the process of making a decision will be distracted from the all-important decision at hand and turn their minds to the activity around them. By having the people remain seated, the preacher can make clear what the response is to be for, and then he can ask the congregation to arise, sing, and respond accordingly.

PROCEDURES OF EVANGELISTIC INVITATIONS

Allow sufficient time. The evangelist must not rush into or out of the giving of the invitation. If the invitation has been built into the central thrust of the message, adequate time will have been allowed for it, even if such planning requires that the body of the sermon be shortened, the announcements eliminated, or one congregational hymn omitted. Such actions ahead of time will help the preacher build to a persuasive and planned climax.

Not only must the evangelist take pains to plan the proper amount of time for the invitation, he must also be sensitive so that he concludes the invitation when it becomes evident that the Spirit of God has stopped calling individuals. No minister should presume on God's rights by lingering and holding on when no visible responses are made.

Follow general guidelines. The following guidelines should control effective evangelistic invitation.

The invitation should be given cautiously.
The invitation should be given clearly.
The invitation should be given compassionately.
The invitation should be given confidently.
The invitation should be given with conviction, not out of conformity to tradition.

The invitation should be given courageously.

The invitation should be given courteously. No undue pressure should be brought to bear upon an individual, making him incapable of reaching a rational decision on the basis of his own volition.

The invitations should be given with dependence upon the Holy Spirit. The serious, responsible evangelist must abandon all professional gimmicks and psychological tricks. He must give the invitation out of a confident trust in the power of a limitless God.

The invitation should be given earnestly.

The invitation should be given with expectancy.

The invitation should be given firmly, with no fumbling or timidity.

The invitation should be given in a friendly manner, not oratorically.

The invitation should be given gently, with no high-pressure techniques or dominating methods.

The invitation should be given with absolute integrity. Make the implications clear-cut. Do not be guilty of saying, "We shall sing only one more verse," and then sing five more.

The invitation should be given prayerfully.

The invitation should be given resourcefully. Change our methods of giving the invitation. Surprise people with something new from time to time.

The invitation should be given scripturally. Quote the Scriptures freely and rely upon the Word to accomplish the divine purpose.

The invitation should be given with urgency and definiteness.

This then should be concluded: The sermonic invitation, to be persuasive, must be intimately tied to the biblical message of the preaching portion. It must be well planned and well thought out. Furthermore, the invitation should focus on specific appeals the preacher chooses ahead of time on the basis of the needs of his congregation. But, most importantly, it must be issued in love and in complete reliance on the Holy Spirit.

ABOVE ALL ELSE

THE POWER OF THE SPIRIT

A sermon may be constructed after the best models; it may conform to all the rules of homiletics; the text may be suitable and fruitful; the plan may be faultless; the execution may discover genius and judgment; there may be accurate analysis and strong reasoning; proof and motive; solidarity and beauty; logic and passion; argument direct and indirect; perspicuity, purity, correctness, propriety, precision; description, antithesis, metaphor, allegory, comparison; motives from goodness, motives from happiness, motives from self-love; appeals to the sense of the beautiful, the sense of right, to the affections, the passions, the emotions;—a sermon may be all this, and yet that very sermon, even though it fell from the lips of a prince of pulpit oratory, were as powerless in the renewal of a soul as in raising the dead, if unaccompanied by the omnipotent energy of the Holy Ghost.[32]

THE COMING OF THE LORD

> Toil on, faint not, keep watch, and pray,
> Be wise the erring soul to win;
> Go forth into the world's highway.
> Compel the wanderer to come in.
> Toil on, and in thy toil rejoice,
> For toil comes rest, for exile's home;
> Soon shalt thou hear the Bridegroom's voice,
> The midnight peal, Behold I come.

Horatius Bonar

NOTES

1. John W. Etter, *The Preacher and His Sermon* (Dayton: United Brethren, 1891), p. 236.
2. Frederick E. Taylor, *The Evangelistic Church* (Philadelphia: Judson, 1927), pp. 125-52.
3. Andrew W. Blackwood, *Evangelism in the Home Church* (New York: Abingdon-Cokesbury, 1942), p. 70.
4. Ozora S. Davis, *Evangelistic Preaching* (New York: Revell, 1921), p. 61.
5. Whitesell, *Evangelistic Preaching and the Old Testament*, pp. 2-8.
6. Brown, *A Quest for Reformation in Preaching*, pp. 140-42.
7. Ibid., pp. 141-42.
8. John Wesley, *Wesley's Standard Sermons* (London: Epworth, 1921), p. 30; see also William Barclay, *Fishers of Men* (Philadelphia: Westminster, 1966), p. 102.
9. T. L. Cuyler, "The Successful Minister," in *Eminent Authors on Effective Revival Preaching*, ed. Walter P. Doe (Providence, R.I.: A. C. Green, 1876), p. 127.
10. Charles B. Templeton, *Evangelism for Tomorrow* (New York: Harper, 1957), pp. 103-4.
11. Lewis O. Brastow, *The Work of the Preacher: A Study of Homiletical Principles and Methods* (Boston: Pilgrim, 1914), p. 247.
12. Charles G. Finney, *Lectures on Revivals of Religion* (New York: Revell, 1868), p. 193.
13. Henry Sloane Coffin, *What to Preach* (New York: George H. Doran, 1930), p. 180.
14. Brastow, *The Work of the Preacher*, pp. 246-47.
15. Charles L. Goodell, *Pastoral and Personal Evangelism* (New York: Revell, 1907), p. 108.
16. Coffin, *What to Preach*, pp. 181-82.
17. Albert Barnes, "Clearness of Style in Preaching," in *Eminent Authors*, p. 68.
18. James Porter, *Revivals of Religion* (New York: Nelson & Phillips, 1877), p. 78.
19. Finney, *Lectures on Revivals*, p. 193.
20. Ibid., p. 192.

21. Coffin, *What to Preach*, p. 182.
22. Blackwood, *Evangelism in the Home Church*, p. 86.
23. Ibid., p. 88.
24. J. Daniel Baumann, *An Introduction to Contemporary Preaching* (Grand Rapids: Baker, 1972), p. 209.
25. Davis, *Evangelistic Preaching*, p. 67.
26. Leighton Ford, *The Christian Persuader* (New York: Harper & Row, 1966), p. 124.
27. Faris D. Whitesell, *Sixty-Five Ways to Give Evangelistic Invitations* (Grand Rapids: Zondervan, 1945), p. 17.
28. D. Martyn Lloyd-Jones, *Preaching and Preachers* (Grand Rapids: Zondervan, 1971), p. 270.
29. Ford, *The Christian Persuader*, pp. 122-23.
30. George E. Sweazey, *Effective Evangelism: The Greatest Work in the World* (New York: Harper, 1953), pp. 60-69.
31. V. L. Stanfield, *Effective Evangelistic Preaching* (Grand Rapids: Baker, 1965), p. 32.
32. Henry C. Fish, *Handbook of Revivals* (Boston: James H. Earle, 1874), p. 281.

BIBLIOGRAPHY

Autry, C. E. *Basic Evangelism*. Grand Rapids: Zondervan, 1959.

Baumann, J. Daniel. *An Introduction to Contemporary Preaching*. Grand Rapids: Baker, 1972.

Benson, Dennis. *Electric Evangelism*. New York: Abingdon, 1973.

Blackwood, Andrew W. *Evangelism in the Home Church*. New York: Abingdon, 1942.

Bromhall, A. J. *Time for Action*. Chicago: InterVarsity, 1965.

* Criswell, W. A. *Criswell's Guide for Pastors*. Nashville: Broadman, 1980.

Davis, Ozora S. *Evangelistic Preaching*. New York: Revell, 1921.

Dobbins, Gaines S. *Evangelism According to Christ*. New York: Harper, 1949.

* Ford, Leighton. *The Christian Persuader*. New York: Harper, 1966.

Fosdick, Henry E. "What's the Matter with Preaching?" In *Re-thinking Evangelism*, edited by George G. Hunter. Nashville: Tidings, 1971.

Green, Bryan. *The Practice of Evangelism*. New York: Scribner's, 1951.

Hale, Joe. *Design for Evangelism*. Nashville: Tidings, 1969.

Hjertman, Wendell E. "The Pastor as His Own Pulpit Evangelist." Th. M. thesis, Northern Baptist Theological Seminary, 1962.

* Lloyd-Jones, D. Martyn. *Preaching and Preachers*. Grand Rapids: Zondervan, 1972.

Packer, J. I. *Evangelism and the Sovereignty of God*. Downers Grove, Ill.: InterVarsity, 1961.

* Perry, Lloyd and John R. Strubhar. *Evangelistic Preaching*. Chicago: Moody, 1979.

Rice, Merton S. "Evangelism and the Pulpit." In *Are You an Evangelist?* edited by Edwin H. Hughes. Nashville: Abingdon-Cokesbury, 1936.

Short, Roy H. *Evangelistic Preaching*. Nashville: Tidings, 1946.* Sith, Bailey E. *Real Evangelistic Preaching*. Nashville: Broadman, 1981.

Stafield, V. L. *Effective Evangelistic Preaching*. Grand Rapids: Baker, 1965.

* Streett, R. Alan. *The Effective Invitation*. Old Tapan, N. J.: Revell, 1984.

Sweazy, George E. *Effective Evangelism: The Greatest Work in the World*. New York: Harper, 1953.

* Walker, Alan. *Evangelistic Preaching*. Grand Rapids: Zondervan, 1988.

Whitesell, Faris D. *Sixty-Five Ways to Give Evangelistic Invitations*. Grand Rapids: Zondervan, 1945.

JOURNAL ARTICLES

Brunsting, Bernard. "Evangelistic Preaching." *Christianity Today* 7 (November 9, 1962): 120-22.

Nogosek, Robert J. "For a Renewal of Preaching." *Worship* 38 (April 1964): 283-88.

"U.S. Congress on Evangelism: A Turning Point?" *Christianity Today* 14 (October 10, 1969): 28-29.

Wetherspoon, J. B. "The Evangelistic Sermon." *Review and Expositor* 64 (January 1945): 59-67.

APPENDIX

SERMON IDEAS FOR A YEAR IN THE WORD

JANUARY

Life at the Crossroads
Deuteronomy 1:19-40

How to Measure Life
Jeremiah 1:1-19

Praying According to Pattern
Matthew 6:1-13

God's Outlook on Life
Mark 8:27–9:1

This Is Life
Philippians 1:12-26

Questions at the Border
1 John 3:1-24

Living with Our Limitations
2 Corinthians 12:1-10

The Tragedy of a Forgotten Promise
Judges 16:13-25

Marvelous Grace
Luke 15

True to His Trust
Genesis 50:15-26

FEBRUARY

Hope Within the Veil
Hebrews 5:11–6:20

The Witness of a Life
Acts 6:1-15

Life's First Lesson
Exodus 20:1-3

Sermons We See
James 1:1-27

Maintaining Godliness in Ungodly
Surroundings
Daniel 6:1-23

The Peril of Neglect
Hebrews 2:1-4

No Money But a Name
Acts 3:1-10

Facing Life's Disappointments
Exodus 15:22-27

MARCH

Christian Harmony
Philippians 2:1-13

The Mystery of Godliness
1 Timothy 3:1-16

Revelations in the Rock
Isaiah 26:4

Triumph or Tragedy
Luke 19:28-40

If You Are Thirsty
John 7:27-52

Life's Inconsistencies
John 13:21-30

What Shall I Do with Jesus?
Matthew 27:11-28

The Parable of the Palm Tree
Psalm 92

APRIL

Because Christ Lives
1 Corinthians 15

Marks of Maturity
1 Corinthians 13

Who Is in Charge?
Jonah 1:1-16

It Is Time for a Change
Jonah 3:1-10

A Demonstration of the Resurrection
Colossians 3:1-17

Contacting for Christ
John 1:35-42 (6:5-14; 12:20-22)

The Blessings of Affliction
Jonah 1:17–2:10

Life Is Worth Living
Jonah 4:1-11

MAY

Confusion at Communion
2 Corinthians 11:17-33

The Spirit-filled Church
Acts 2

Mrs. Far-Above-Rubies
Proverbs 31:10-31

The Church: The Body of Christ
1 Corinthians 12:1-31

Stones of Remembrance
Joshua 4:6-24

Freedom from Fear
Revelation 1:9-20

The Bush Is Burning Again
Exodus 3:1-12

The Influence of a Christian Life
Matthew 5:1-16

Christianity's Conflict with Religion
Acts 19:8-20

That's All I Want
Psalm 23

JUNE

Forgiven
Psalm 103

Entrusted with the Gospel
1 Thessalonians 2:1-12

Transmission Trouble
2 Timothy 2:1-26

The School of Suffering
Job 42:1-9

Crowned Before the King
Hebrews 12:1-17

Souls at Sea
Acts 27:1–28:14

Taming the Tongue
James 3:1-12

The Battle Is the Lord's
1 Samuel 17:32-51

Christian Profession and Partiality
    James 2
	Glimpses of Glory
	    Revelation 21:1–22:5

NOVEMBER

God's Completed Work
    John 19:30
	Son of Encouragement
	    Acts 4:32-37

Citizenship in Heaven's Glory
    Philippians 1:27-30; 3:17-21
	A Call to Conflict
	    Ephesians 6:10-20

Praise from a Pardoned People
    Psalm 103
	A Recipe for Thanksgiving
	    1 Thessalonians 5:16-18

More Than Conquerors
    Romans 8:18-39
	Revival Through the Word
	    2 Chronicles 34:14-21

DECEMBER

God's Peace
    John 14:27
	A Friend of God
	    James 2:23

Getting Ready for Christmas
    Luke 3:1-6
	The Wisdom of Waiting
	    Isaiah 40:30-31

When Christmas Comes to Working People
    Luke 2:1-20
	The Cost of Christmas
	    Matthew 2:1-15

God First
    Matthew 6:19-34
	Preparation for the Journey
	    Joshua 3:1-6

INDEX

Moody Press, a ministry of Moody Bible Institute, is designed for education, evangelization, and edification. If we may assist you in knowing more about Christ and the Christian life, please write us without obligation: Moody Press, c/o MLM, Chicago, Illinois 60610.